P9-DUT-821

Creature Comforts

A Quilter's Animal Alphabet Book

Marie Shirer   **Barbara Brackman**

Cover Design: Geri Wolfe Boesen
Interior Layout: Anthony Jacobson
Illustrations: Marla Gibbs Stefanelli

On the Cover: Panda-Panda made by Marie Shirer.
Photograph by Jerry DeFelice.

ISBN 0-87069-455-3

Library of Congress Catalog
Card Number 85-050923

Copyright©1986
Wallace-Homestead Book Company

All rights reserved. No part of this publication may be
reproduced, stored in a retrieval system, or transmitted in
any form or by any means, electronic, mechanical, photo-
copying, recording or otherwise, without prior permission of
the copyright owner or the publisher.

10 9 8 7 6 5 4 3

Published by

Wallace-Homestead Book Company
580 Waters Edge
Lombard, Illinois 60148

One of the

ABC PUBLISHING abc
Companies

To Sadie and Spot,
our favorite objets d'arf.

Contents

Acknowledgments

Our thanks to Cuesta Benberry, Susan Bengtson, Karey Bresenhan, Joyce Gross, Betty Gustafson, Mrs. W. A. Hudgins, Bonnie Leman, *Quilter's Newsletter Magazine*, Linda Reuther, Helen Rose, Julie Silber, Cathy Smith, Sandra Todaro, Louise O. Townsend, and Shelly Zegart for help in finding old quilts, patterns, and information about them.

To Grace Simpson Caudill, Linda Emery, Marci Francisco, and Rebecca Shirer for allowing us to give patterns based on their designs.

To Kathy Dubois for checking yardage figures in the project directions.

To the makers and owners of all the animal quilts shown in this book, who share our enjoyment of creature comforts.

Introduction

Our interest in the kingdom of patchwork animals began a few years ago when Marie decided to piece a zoo quilt for a soon-to-be-born niece. She asked Barbara for help in locating quilt patterns for pieceable creatures. We checked files of patterns clipped from old magazines and newspapers, scanned picture books for old animal quilts, and corresponded with pattern collectors. After several months of looking, we realized, to our surprise, that pieced animal patterns were scarce.

Of the patterns we found, few, in our opinion, achieved the right balance between practicality and good design. Some were easy enough to piece, but they failed to capture the personality of the animal; others were expressive, but impossible or impractical to sew. And some were just ridiculous. We modified a few of the impractical patterns to make them pieceable, added some details to the overly simple designs, and began designing our own. Why not a pieced armadillo or stegosaurus? How about a zebra? Perhaps even a yak! It seemed that any animal could be pieced. By then we were hooked; thus, this book.

The pieced animal quilt has obvious appeal—not only to the children for whom many of the old patterns were originally designed, but also to quiltmakers who prefer piecing to appliqué. These patterns also are enchanting to all of us grown-ups who haven't outgrown our delight in bears, pigs, cats, and other members of the animal world. Depending on their size and color scheme, quilts pieced from these patterns can decorate nurseries, country kitchens, or office waiting rooms. The images so popular for decorating in the 1980s—the Scotties and sheep, bears and geese—are all pieceable. We offer many ideas for incorporating animals in a variety of patchwork projects, and you will undoubtedly dream up many more.

In addition to ideas, we offer fifty scaled block designs arranged to form a complete alphabet of animal designs. These blocks can be easily enlarged or reduced to any size you need. Most of the fifty blocks are original designs or adaptations of the patterns we found in early twentieth-century publications. A few, too good to change, are exact reproductions of old patterns. The difficulty levels of the blocks range from beginner to expert. Beginner designs (the blackbird, the two cows, the mouse, and several others) include only a few pattern pieces and simple angles. More complex designs (the camel and the monkey, for example) have numerous pieces and require setting in angled patches. Some patterns lend themselves to machine piecing, but all the blocks can be sewn with hand stitching.

The thirteen projects also vary in complexity. The Scottie Quilt and Grazing Cows are quite easy to make, while The Zoo Quilt is a real challenge. Many of the animal designs, made from a single block with a simple border, are effective as wall hangings. You'll find patterns and directions for small theme quilts using just a few animals blocks, such as Noah's Ark. The fifty block designs are modular, so you can send Noah off with a kangaroo and a zebra, or maybe a panda and a pig.

Choose any number of inhabitants for your version of The Zoo, or select one animal for each letter to make a twin-size Animal Alphabet Quilt. For some letters you'll have several animals from which to choose; for others there is only one.

Once you have looked through our sampler of designs, you may get the urge to draft your own favorite creature. We have included instructions on how to draw pieced animals (Chapter 2), and we encourage you to try it even if you have little confidence in your artistic talents. The techniques Marie has developed for designing a pieceable kingdom have worked well in classes we have taught. Quiltmakers who were afraid to draft a nine-patch pattern have completed portraits on paper and in piecework.

We hope you enjoy our pieceable animals, whether you're sewing for a little one or for yourself. Hopefully, you'll find the hardest part is deciding which animal to stitch first. Wherever you begin, enjoy!

1
Historical Pieced Animals

Patchwork patterns are an evolving art form. And on the evolutionary scale, pieced animals are a late development. The majority of the designs date from the years 1928–1940, which were the peak of the quiltmaking fad that flared between the wars. But decades earlier, two late nineteenth-century trends led to the appearance of the pieced animal designs. The first was a taste for realism in quilt design, which is so apparent in appliquéd and embroidered quilts, but is also evident in pieced work. The other fashion was the child's quilt, depicting the world of nursery rhymes, toys, and pets.

Realistic Subject Matter

Naturalistic patchwork was the exception rather than the rule in the nineteenth century, when the majority of quilt patterns passed on in the folk tradition were abstract rather than realistic. Quiltmakers working with pieced patterns were limited to some degree by geometry, but fashion also dictated a non-figurative style. The exceptions included the stylized pieced baskets, trees, and houses that appeared mid-century. The doves that hovered in quilted windows were symbolized in diamonds, and the flying geese passed by in formations pieced only of triangles. Even appliqué, with its potential for realistic detail, leaned toward an abstract version of the natural world. Occasionally, an artist might depict a particular house or dog or civic monument, as in the Baltimore Album quilts, but the appliquéd patterns that appeared over and over were mere suggestions of actual flora and fauna.

In the last quarter of the nineteenth century, patterns became more representational. Ruth Finley, an early quilt historian, noted the change in her 1929 book, *Old Patchwork Quilts and the Women Who Made Them*. In a chapter pessimistically entitled "The Decline of Handicraft," she cited the popularity in the 1870s of the Little Red Schoolhouse, the Fan, and the Crazy Quilt as evidence of the trend towards representative patterns. Finley's inclusion of crazy quilts in the realistic category is appropriate, since their popularity did have a strong influence. The throws made of satin and velvet scraps with fussily embroidered pictures encouraged a style in which detail and realism were highly valued.

Another related style was the outline-embroidered quilt, in which line drawings were stitched (usually with red floss) on white cotton or linen. Popular subject matter for the outline-embroidered quilts, as well as for the crazy quilts, were the Kate Greenaway figures—boys and girls in eighteenth-century costume, designed by the English illustrator of children's books. The detailed motifs were adapted to outline embroidery as early as 1880, when the December issue of *Peterson's Magazine* said, "Just at present such a style of embroidery is very much the fashion and it has the advantage of being very effective, very rapidly done, and very cheap." Thereafter, the Greenaway children, with an occasional pet, were a fixture in all types of Victorian fancywork, including quilts.

Around the turn of the century, the Greenaway children were supplanted by Bertha Corbett's simpler and more stylized Sunbonnet Children, whose appeal continued as the fad for crazy quilts died. The costumed children helped create a market for pictorial embroidered quilts. That market grew throughout the first half of the twentieth century, with periodicals and pattern houses prospering by selling designs as diverse as flowers and Bible stories, fruit, and state birds, all rendered in realistic detail.

In the early decades of the twentieth century, the embroidered Sunbonnet Children were adapted to appliqué techniques. An early appearance in print was a pastel version designed by Marie D. Webster for a *Ladies' Home Journal* article in 1912. The subsequent popularity of appliquéd Sunbonnet Children strongly influenced the market for pictorial appliqué. In her position as needlework editor at

Ladies' Home Journal, Webster influenced not only the Sunbonnet Sue fad but, with designs such as her sunflower and poppy quilts, she shaped the pictorial appliqué style that flowered in the 1930s. Anne Orr, her counterpart at *Good Housekeeping,* developed a style of realistic quilt, although she specialized in pieced work. Her subtly shaded floral designs were based on a grid-like mosaic of squares and triangles, a technique she adapted from cross-stitch and needlepoint charts.

Webster and Orr were among the first quilt pattern designers, creating a new occupation. Nineteenth-century quiltmakers had used the patterns that had sprung up as folklore without benefit of professional designers. The gradual change to commercial sources began in the 1880s, when magazines began advocating styles such as the Crazy Quilt and offering patterns designed by professional illustrators. Webster and Orr, with their signature styles, completed the change to commercial sources. They changed the way patterns were shared and the way they looked, developing styles influenced by the decorative arts

of the time. Webster's appliqué designs borrowed the sinuous natural style of Art Noveau. Orr's pieced designs were derived from the geometric fragmentation of natural forms popularized by the Arts and Crafts movement, Cubism, and Art Deco.

Designers, with their knowledge of mainstream art, developed a pattern style more sophisticated than the traditional folk art patterns. While some of the twentieth-century designers continued to draw in the manner of the nineteenth-century patterns, many like Orr and Webster broke away from the past, adding more naturalism. With their knowledge of the principles of abstract art, they could easily interpret nature in shapes that were possible to piece in fabric. Some, like Orr, rendered animals in simple squares and triangles. M. Buren, who designed the "Prudence Penny" patterns, and the as yet anonymous designers known as Alice Brooks and Laura Wheeler, fragmented nature into a variety of shapes. Once Picasso could interpret the human face as a series of planes, Prudence Penny could, at a more mundane level, interpret a hippopotamus

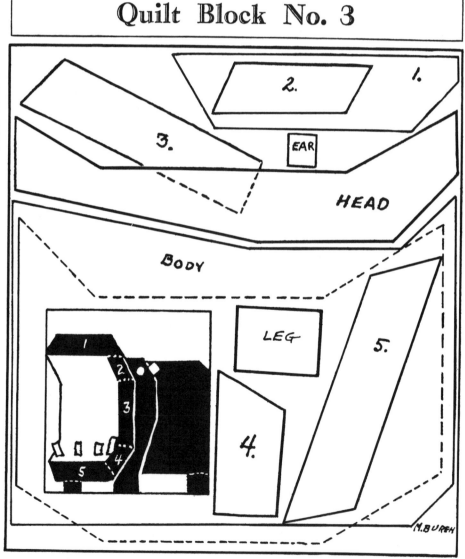

HERE'S HOW--NOW BUILD MR. HIPPO

The hippo's back is fine for fleas
To romp on at their leisure.
He never counts his calories,
But eats his food with pleasure.

How to put hippopotamus together—
The large piece indicated by dotted lines is the inside of the mouth, pieces 1 to 5 are sewed to this. The head piece comes next, then the large body piece is sewed on next. Legs are cut as indicated, the front leg however, is only half as long as the other two. Ear, teeth and eye are appliqued on and the whole design is sewed to a nine-inch square or directly onto the quilt. Allow for seams when cutting.

This is Number 3 of the series of quilt blocks in Prudence Penny's Patchwork Zoo which are being published each Sunday and Wednesday in the Post-Intelligencer. If you have missed some of those already printed, send in the following coupon.

PRUDENCE PENNY,

Post-Intelligencer, Seattle.

Please send me the miniature of twenty animals and numbers 1 and 2.

Name ....

Address ....

City ....

Hippopotamus pattern from "Prudence Penny's Patchwork Zoo," Seattle Post-Intelligencer, *1933*

in geometric pieces of cloth. It may be that there were no nineteenth-century pieced animal quilts because nineteenth-century folk artists did not have the abstract vision that we of the twentieth century take for granted.

Children's Quilts

While the taste for realism in quiltmaking led to a style of piecing easily adaptable to animals, the fashion for children's quilts demanded animals as subject matter. Children's quilts were a late-Victorian trend, growing from the belief that childhood was a special time, separate from adulthood. The earlier concept of the child as a small version of the adult is reflected in cradle quilts of the nineteenth century, which were cut or scaled-down versions of the patterns used in adults' quilts.

Once the concept of the child as an individual with special needs and interests developed, the sentimental Victorians seized upon the idea. The popularity of the Kate Greenaway figures is evidence of their reverence for childhood, as is the appearance of the child's quilt especially designed for the child's taste (or the adult's interpretation of what that taste might be). From the beginning, animals were pictured. An "amusing" appliqué or embroidered child's quilt was described in the *Dorcus Magazine of Woman's Handiwork* in August 1886. Noah's Ark quilts were a "fashionable little 'fad' of the day in fancywork." (Contemporary evidence of this fad in the form of handed-down quilts is lacking, however.) The seamstress was to copy pairs of animals from picture books and appliqué them in Turkey Red twill or embroider them in cross stitch, crewel, or couching.

The Young Ladies Journal of December 1889 offered a pattern for an appliquéd nursery rug or cot counterpane featuring images of animals and a clown. In 1912, *The Ladies' Home Journal* summarized the theme of the crib quilt: "Children while very young show marked preference for certain toys and little belongings and, could they have their very own, they would love them dearly."

From the beginning, the animals in children's quilts tended to the domesticated variety. An early exception was a 1907 *Ladies' Home Journal* pattern for appliquéd "Tito," a wolf or coyote baying at the moon. Tito was unique in that he was neither a cuddly nursery pet nor a farm animal, but a wild beast with appeal for older children. Although he was followed by many more patterns for animal quilts, the later examples were designed with younger children in mind. By the 1920s, the animals to be embroidered or appliquéd on children's quilts were best described as "cute." Typical is a 1935 *Capper's Weekly* column describing a "Crib Quilt of Sleepy-Time Pets," appliquéd with a "Playful pup, a meow kitty, a curly-tailed pig, and a peep-peep chick." The animals were as coy as their descriptions. Their large heads, plump bodies, and long lashes implied, as did the copy, that the quilt was specifically for the very young.

Pieced Animals

The earliest pieced animal quilt we have found is in Shelly Zegart's collection. She has a cow pieced of squares and triangles in turn-of-the-century fabrics. Her horse (see Color Section), made of a mosaic of squares, looks to be a little later. Both quilts are full-sized and thus probably were not designed for young children. Since we have found no published sources for the designs, we conclude that they are folk patterns—possibly one-of-a-kind creations.

A crib quilt with an elephant, giraffe, and cat pieced in the square-and-triangle method, attributed to the year 1910, has been pictured in several recent publications, including Woodard and Greenstein's *Crib Quilts and Other Small Wonders.* "The Circus Quilt" is in the collection of Karey Bresenhan. Family history states that her grand-

CAPPER'S WEEKLY, NOVEMBER 2, 1935.

Crib Quilt of Sleepy Time Pets

Delightful friends for the little feller's sleepy time are these barnyard pets—leastwise most of them will stand the "barny" classification. Favorite friends they soon will be anyhow, if you make them all into a crib quilt for the littlest one's bed. There are eight of these little animals, each one to be appliqued on a quilt block. There's a frisky squirrel, a playful pup, a meow kitty, a curly-tailed pig, a carrot-eating bunny, a quack-quack duck, a peep-peep chick, and a funny running bear. All come stamped on nine-inch blocks of nice white quiltex material and applique patches for making them are stamped on soft yellow material just ready to cut and whip into place. There are also directions for doing the work included in our package No. B-4—and would you believe it, the makings for this cunning crib quilt will cost you only 25 cents. Of course, you'll want to make some youngster happy at Christmas time. Order the package from Needlework Service, Capper's Weekly, Topeka, Kan.

"A Crib Quilt of Sleepy-Time Pets," from Capper's Weekly, *1935*

9

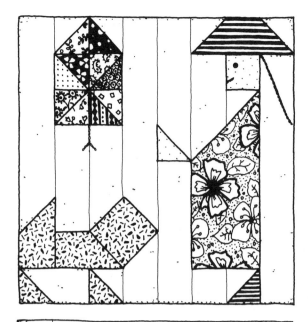

Clipping from Needlecraft Magazine, 1928

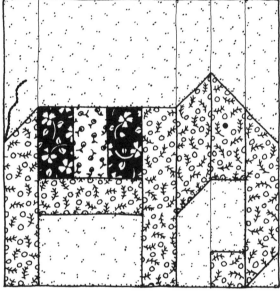

Blocks from "Paper, Paint, and Patchwork," designed by Ruth B. Oppenheimer and Wilhemine Haas, Woman's Home Companion, 1928

mother, Myrtle Augusta Patterson, made it for the birth of Karey's father in 1910. But discovery of a similar quilt (see Color Section), owned by Cathy Smith, and closely related patterns dated 1928 indicate that "The Circus Quilt" probably dates from 1928 or later, contemporary to the other pieced animal crib quilts we have found. That there are at least two such similar quilts indicates that Mrs. Patterson used a commercial pattern, but the source is still a mystery. Both Karey Bresenhan's quilt and Cathy Smith's quilt bear a close resemblance to the design style of Ruth B. Oppenheimer and Wilhemine Haas, whose pillow and crib quilt projects were featured in *Needlecraft Magazine* in March 1928, and in *Woman's Home Companion* in November of that year. It is possible that Oppenheimer and Haas designed these animals.

Because we have found so few actual quilts in pieced animal designs, it is easier to trace their history through published patterns. The 1928 Oppenheimer/Haas designs appear to be the first patterns for pieced animals. The *Needlecraft* article heralds "Patchwork in a New Form," and it may be that these designers did create the pieced animal style. Over the next decade or so, a few other designers contributed animal patterns, refining the style. While the appliquéd and embroidered animal designs of the 1920s and 1930s seemed to grow more infantile, the pieced animals grew more sophisticated, appealing to adults and older children as well as to toddlers. It may be that cuteness is more difficult to render in piecework. Whatever the reason, the pieced animals do have a more universal appeal. Contrast the "peep-peep chick" with the dapper penguin brothers in "Prudence Penny's Patchwork Zoo."

Possibly their lack of cuteness banished these pieced animals to the obscurity from which we resurrect them. Relatively few were published, and few actually were made into quilts. But it wasn't only aesthetics that made these hard-edge animals wallflowers. Most were poorly designed for quiltmaking. The pattern designers of the 1920s and 1930s seemed to know more about abstract design than about quilt construction. The animals themselves were effectively designed from shapes that could be more or less easily pieced, but most designers refused to deal with a pieced background. They advised the seamstress to piece the animal and then appliqué it to a square block. Omitting the background piecing required less newsprint, since few pattern pieces had to be included. But whether it was

Prudence Penny's Patchwork Zoo

Animal blocks labeled: KANGAROO, CAMEL, HIPPOPOTAMUS, REINDEER, SEAL, ZEBRA, SQUIRREL, BUFFALO, FOX, LION, GIRAFFE, WILD CAT, ELEPHANT, CROCODILE, POLAR BEAR, MONKEY, BEAVER, PENGUINS, OSTRICH, LEOPARD

LION, LEOPARD PARADE ACROSS PIECED QUILTS

Prudence Penny's Patchwork Zoo, sixth quilt pattern to be published in the Post-Intelligencer, will appear one block each Wednesday and Sunday until the complete set of twenty blocks has appeared. After time has been allowed to finish the quilts, a contest will be held to choose the best quilts made from this pattern.

Each block is nine inches square when finished and represents an animal from the Zoo. Blocks to appear will give patterns for pieces, full sized, so the quilt maker may cut her designs and with the aid of the descriptive text be able to assemble the various pieces into a complete design.

The completed quilt will be a combination of applique and pieced work to make an interesting and attractive gift for grownups or youngsters. Remember to watch for the first block to appear next Wednesday.

"Prudence Penny's Patchwork Zoo," Seattle Post-Intelligencer, *1933*

editorial economy or ignorance of quiltmaking that dictated the technique, there is something unsatisfactory as well as inefficient in appliquéing several triangles to a background square.

Artist Eveline Foland of *The Kansas City Star* was one of the few designers who dealt with the background. She designed an elephant named Ararat and a donkey called Giddap (see Color Section) from squares and triangles during the election year of 1931. In 1936, *Star* illustrator Edna Marie Dunn borrowed the style and Foland's characteristic triangular toes to design a dog. These three pieced animals turn up occasionally in quilts in the Midwest, testimony to the popularity of the *Star* quilt column.

Other square and triangle designs from the time include "An Appealing Child's Quilt" (*Good Housekeeping* pamphlet #A-1302) by Anne Orr, and Lockport Batting's "Slumberland Quilt," from which the border on Rebecca Shirer's "Stormstown Cows" (see Color Section) is taken.

In 1933, the Prudence Penny column, which was often signed M. Buren, ran the series called "The Patchwork Zoo" in the *Seattle Post-Intelligencer*. The inhabitants were to be pieced and then appliquéd to a background, but unlike the square and triangle patterns, they were composed of a variety of shapes, including curves, for a more naturalistic appearance. Around the same time, the Needlecraft Company, a syndicated pattern source, sold several pieced animals through its Alice Brooks and Laura Wheeler columns. A cat, a flying bird, a robin, and two Scottie dogs are perhaps the most sophisticated of the pieced animals

A SWOPE PARK ELEPHANT FIGURES IN A QUILT BLOCK.

ARARAT

23 PURPLE / 30 GOLD
7 PURPLE / 46 GOLD / 37 WHITE
17 WHITE

Eveline Foland

(Clip and save.)

Little did Ararat, slow old elephant that he is, ever think he would find himself gracing a quilt block when he came to live in the Swope Park zoo, there to become enthroned in the hearts of Kansas City children. Here he is, nevertheless, and it is surpris-ing how dignified and important he will look ambling across a quilt for little brother's bed. Big sister could make it, too, now that school is over, for it is not a difficult piece of quilting.

One thinks of purple and gold as colors, because they are royal colors, and in the far East royalty traveled on elephants, but dark blocks with a bright blanket would be quite as pretty. Piece in rows and follow pattern when setting together. A generous strip of white should be used between the blocks, which are 21 by 13½ inches. Allow for seams.

(Copyright, 1931, by The Kansas City Star.)

Ararat pattern designed by Eveline Foland, 1931, first published in The Kansas City Star

of the era since they include a variety of shapes, curved piecing, and pieced backgrounds.

In the 1920s and 1930s, nearly every pattern source offered a pieced butterfly design. The earliest we have found is dated 1928, designed by Verdie Foster for *Needlecraft Magazine*. She claimed she was the first to design a butterfly in "old-time" pieced work, but she was certainly not the last. The butterfly's popularity may be attributed to the fact that the wings offered the scrap quilt enthusiast a spot for a variety of colorful prints. A butterfly sold in the 1930s under the Laura Wheeler signature combined two scrap quilt fads—each butterfly wing includes a fan design.

By the 1940s, enthusiasm for quiltmaking had faded and patterns gradually disappeared from magazines and newspapers. During the 1950s and 1960s, only an occasional new pattern for a pieced animal appeared in print. Several were designed by readers of *Aunt Kate's Quilting Bee*, a small magazine for pattern collectors published in the 1960s and early 1970s. Since the revival of interest in quiltmaking in the 1970s, artists have been emphasizing original designs in quilts, and a few have chosen animals as their subject matter. Ruth McDowell and Pauline Burbidge have directed their impressive piecing skills to animals, rendering lobsters, pelicans, ducks, and scarab beetles in realistic detail.

Using the old patterns we have adapted or the design techniques described in the next chapter, you can piece your own versions of the animal kingdom, adding to one of quiltmaking's more recent traditions.

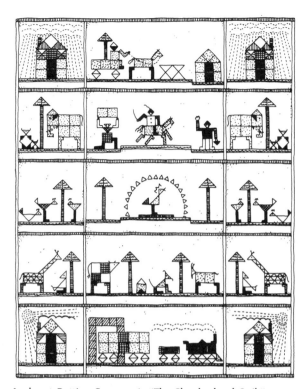

Lockport Batting Company's "The Slumberland Quilt"

Butterflies Glorify a Pieced Quilt— Laura Wheeler Shows How

BUTTERFLY   PATTERN 1408

Butterflies—wings spread for flight—make this most stunning "Nature" quilt. And here's the marvel of it—their wings are composed of otherwise useless scraps—colorful ones, set in, in a fan shape. Here's a wonderfully simple 10 inch block to piece! Lovely when done! Pattern 1408 contains complete, simple instructions for cutting, sewing and finishing, together with yardage chart, diagram of quilt to help arrange the blocks for single and double bed size, and a diagram of block which serves as a guide for placing the patches and suggests contrasting materials.

Send 10 cents in stamps or coin (coin preferred) for this pattern to The **Daily Times, Needlecraft Dept. 82, Eighth Avenue, New York, N. Y.**

Butterfly, Laura Wheeler pattern #1408, Needlecraft Company

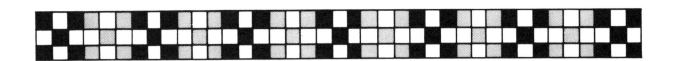

2
Designing Pieced Animals

Almost any animal can be adapted to piecing, although some shapes and sizes will be easier to sew than others. You can design a successful pieced animal using only a few simple shapes, or you can plan a more realistic design with dozens of pieces. There are only a few limitations.

There is one simple "rule" about piecing: *anything you can draw on paper (within reason) can be pieced in fabric.* Some limitations are obvious. For instance, you would probably never attempt to piece a nine-patch with ⅟₁₆″ squares! (We must admit that some of the piecing in the patterns for The Zoo approached that level of ridiculousness, but the blocks were fun to make nevertheless.) A similar construction problem occurs when you have many points coming together at the same place (especially if the patches are small), but that problem is easily avoided when designing animals because you can put the seams wherever you please.

The other design limitation, which is not really a rule but rather a suggestion, is not as obvious or as easy to grasp. *Angled patches usually require a seam at each corner, with the seam being on the side with the wider angle.* That sounds difficult, but a few examples should help. Let's take a look at an old pattern called Simple Five-Point Star.

If this pattern is drawn without seams, it should be obvious that the single star shape would not be easy to piece to the background. It could be appliquéd, but not pieced. Let's divide the star into five diamond-shaped pieces.

That looks better, but once the star is pieced, it will still be difficult to join to the background. Let's try adding a seam at each point of the star and at each indentation.

This drawing looks much better, and now our star block can be pieced easily. However, some of the seams are not necessary (although there is nothing wrong with having all of them there). Let's remove the seams at the star points and see how that looks.

 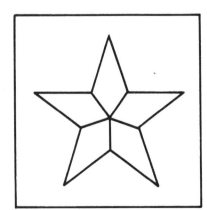 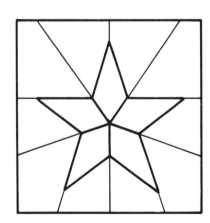

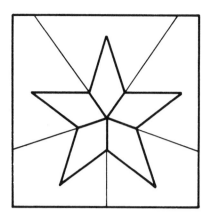

If you have done piecing before, you probably know this example is a difficult, if not impossible, piecing task. Sewing those star points into an angle would probably require a clip in the background fabric at the point, which might weaken the quilt top. It might also create a pucker. Let's put these seams back in, and remove the seams at the indentations of the star.

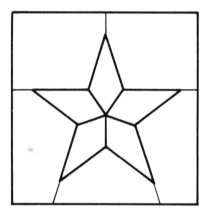

Doesn't that look more pieceable? Now there is a seam in the star at each outside angle of the background pieces, and there is a seam in the background pieces at each outside angle of the star patches. This is the best solution to piecing a five-pointed star into a background fabric.

The same idea will apply to pieced patches with sharp curves. Curved seams such as those in a Drunkard's Path design, or gentler (shallower) curves, will not require a seam in the background patch. Sharp curves such as those in flower petals will probably require a seam at the sharpest part of the curve to allow easy piecing.

So how do five-point stars and flower petals relate to pieced animals? They don't, really, except as an exercise in seams. Remember the rule: Anything that can be drawn on paper, *with seams in the right places*, can be pieced in fabric. Animals (or flowers, or anything else) can be designed in much the same way as stars and flower petals.

You will find that seams are not only a means by which fabric patches are joined, but that they can add greatly to the design. Seams will define body parts (arms, legs, necks, and so on) and will also serve to "fracture" the quilt block into pleasing shapes, especially in the background.

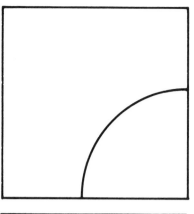

Unlike traditional pieced quilt patterns, many animal blocks will have a different template (or pattern) for every patch in the block. Of course, this does not make piecing animals any more difficult; it simply means that you will have more pattern pieces. It also means that, if you are making only one block, you only have to cut one patch from each pattern piece.

Choosing a Design

Designing your own pieced animal is easy. First, decide which animal you would like to work with. Then find several reasonably accurate drawings or photographs of that animal, or draw an animal yourself. Look for (or draw) a *realistic* version of your subject. Adapting designs for piecework is a form of stylizing, and if you *begin* with a stylized drawing, you might lose the identifiable traits of the species and end up with a generic, unidentifiable animal. Many children's coloring books have drawings that are perfect for adaptation to pieced quilts, with just the right amount of simplification and detail. An excellent book, *How to Draw Animals* by Jack Hamm, can help you learn to recognize basic shapes when drawing animals. Hamm's book is also a good reference for accurate drawings of many animals. Greeting cards, wildlife books, and newspaper and magazine photographs are excellent design sources. The reason for choosing several versions of your subject is that you will more easily identify important traits in your animal. If all of your "originals" of, say, a fox, show white on the belly and tip of tail, you will want to include that feature in your design.

If you want to adapt a cartoon-type design, find several examples from which to work. These funny-paper designs, although stylized, are so identifiable that they will probably adapt successfully to patchwork.

One word of advice: Some animal designs will require many more design lines (which means seams to sew) than others. "Chunky" animals may prove to be more simple than those with gangly legs or tendrils. Also, you will find that some perspectives will prove more successful than others. For instance, a side view of a turtle may be better than a front view, but a peacock will look great shown from the front. If you are nervous about your drawing ability, plan to use the same perspective as your "original" (that is, the book or greeting card you are using for reference).

Designing with Simple Shapes

Some animals can be depicted successfully in patchwork with the use of only a few simple shapes. In the Animal Alphabet section of this book you will find a mouse and a blackbird. These two creatures are made of only one or two triangles (with the addition of an embroidered tail, ear, eye, and nose for the mouse). Not all animals can be simplified to that extent, of course, especially if the animal is not readily identifiable. A mouse is easy to spot with its long tail and round ears, so it doesn't matter that a mouse isn't really shaped quite like a triangle. A blackbird, if made from black fabric and shown perched in a tree, can be identified by anyone. However, if we were to design a pieced gnu with a few simple shapes, chances are that the design would not be successful because gnus are not in the public's visual "vocabulary" of animals. Cows, though, are shaped a little like gnus, and we can spot those a mile away.

To design an animal in the ultra-simple style, study a picture of the beast and determine its basic shape(s). For instance, a cow has a square rear end, fairly straight legs, and a flat, squared-off snout. Those features, and little else, are used to depict this version of a cow.

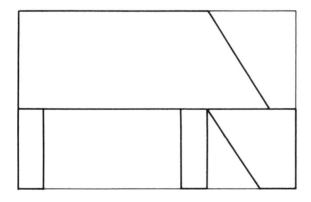

Let's try designing a fish. The basic body shape can be made from a triangle with a smaller triangle added for the tail.

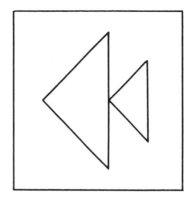

To make the block pieceable, we simply extend some of the fish seam lines to the edge of the block, making sure there is a seam at each angle of the design on the wider side of the angle (as we did for the Five-Pointed Star pattern). Just for fun, let's add some bubbles to be embroidered.

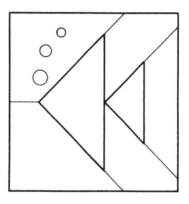

If you want to design animals in a more realistic style, read on!

Realistic Design: Making the Rough Sketch

When designing animals in a realistic style, it is helpful to study the beast (or pictures of it) for a few minutes to notice the important traits. Perhaps you will even want to make a list of distinguishing features, such as body proportions and basic shapes. For instance, you might note that nearly half the height of a giraffe is in the neck. And the upper part of a giraffe's back leg is nearly as wide as the neck. Notes like these will help keep you on track, even if you do not think you have an "artist's eye."

Once you have chosen your subject, selected several versions of your creature to use as "models," and noted the distinguishing features, make a rough sketch in the finished size you want. Please don't let the words "rough sketch" make you nervous. The sketch can be simply a tracing of your original, enlarged if necessary to make your quilt block the right size. A small wall hanging should be worked out full size on graph paper, which can be purchased by the yard from art supply stores. A larger quilt with repeating blocks can be drawn to scale on graph paper with only a single block drafted full size. (If you are a little shaky on enlarging a drawing, see the Appendix for enlarging instructions.) If your enlarged drawing doesn't come out quite right, just tell yourself you have stylized the design. Or, visit your local photocopy store for a mechanically produced enlargement.

With pencil, lightly sketch only the outline, plus any vital body lines, such as legs, arms, and the head. The tendency is to make the drawing too small, so think big and fill the design area. Perhaps you will want to show only the animal's head. Or, maybe you will want to incorporate a tree or other design element. It's okay to have some background showing, but try not to let the design get "lost" in too much background space.

You will want to use a pencil so you can erase and adjust as necessary. If you are planning a pieced border for your quilt, you might want to read that section of this chapter before proceeding since the border can often determine the size of the quilt block.

As you sketch, refer to your list of design characteristics. Is the head too big or too small? Is the neck long enough? Is the tail too long? Body too fat? Too thin? Is the body symmetrical enough (meaning that the left side mirrors the right side)? Stand back and study your animal every few minutes as you work, making changes with pencil, and eventually the design will come into focus for you.

Let's use, as an example, a simple shape like a fish. Here is the rough sketch, shown in miniature to fit the pages of this book.

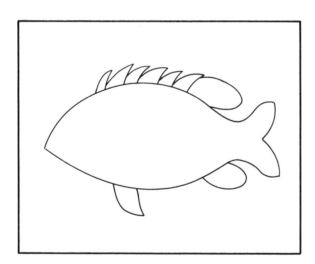

Notice that only the body outline and fins are sketched in. Details such as eyes and scales can be added later, whether they are to be pieced, appliquéd, or embroidered. See how the fish design adequately fills the block? There is still room for us to add sand and perhaps some seaweed, but the fish is not so small that it gets lost in the finished block design.

Marking the Design Lines

The next step is to tentatively mark the design lines, which are the seam lines (sewing lines) of the quilt patches. These design lines can be either straight or curved. Let's use some of each.

Remember that each angle will require a seam in each arm of the angle, plus a seam in the background. Use your lines sparingly! Let's try marking design lines on the body of the fish.

Place a ruler along one of the straighter sides of the fish and mark a line. Move the ruler and *lightly* mark a straight line along the next segment of the fish outline.

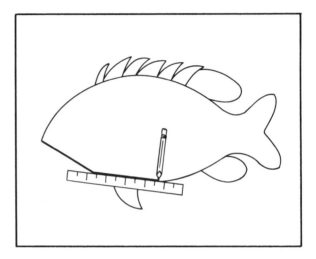

Continue around the fish, making straight lines, until the outline is complete. You may find that you can simplify the shape (and the number of lines) and still retain the shape of the fish without sacrificing any of the design. In fact, you may decide at this point that the style you really want is the simple one with only a few shapes and pattern pieces. It's okay to change your mind!

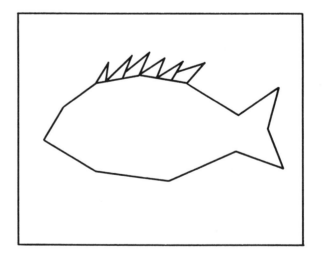

The fins seem like a good place for some gently curving lines.

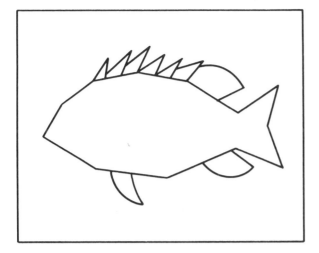

The design lines in the fish can indicate the gills, a fin, and the belly, or they can just be pleasing design lines.

Now it's time to divide the background with seam lines. For now, we will leave the background plain, without sand or seaweed. The seam lines of the background can be placed in many positions. These seam lines can *add to the design of the piece by fracturing the design surface.* Most animals are enhanced with background lines that radiate out from the body as extensions of the seam lines within the animal. Remember the suggestion about having a seam line at each outside (or wide) angle. Refer to the drawings to see good and better examples.

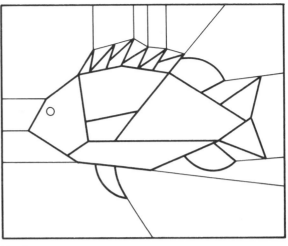

Good

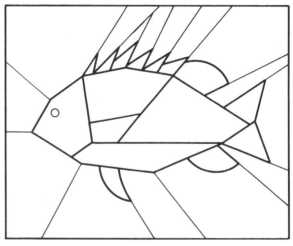

Better

Notice that in each example a seam is placed at every "wide angle," as necessary to construct the block.

Adding Details

Some details are so small that piecing is neither practical nor desirable. Besides, there's no reason why quilt blocks need to be all pieced (or worked exclusively in any technique). The fin on our fish, whether we choose the simple style with only a few pieces or the realistic style with many pieces, could be appliquéd instead of pieced. The eye is a perfect spot for appliqué. If you prefer, the eye and other details can be embroidered. For the Panda-Panda (see Front Cover) the ear, eyes, and nose were appliquéd (with the straight edges inserted in a seam before blindstitching the curved edges). The round patches on the Teddy Bear (see Color Section) were pieced, but they could just as well have been appliquéd. Many of the details on The Zoo were appliquéd or embroidered. Quilting can also complete many details of the quilt design. *Always use the best technique available to achieve the desired effect.*

Another Design Style: Squares and Triangles

Yet another design style—one that has been adopted successfully by quilters for many years—resembles the gridded style of cross-stitch embroidery. Squares and triangles are joined to create animals or other design elements. A number of examples of this simplified design style are shown in Grace Simpson's book *Quilts Beautiful: Their Stories and How to Make Them.* This clever dog is one of Grace's designs.

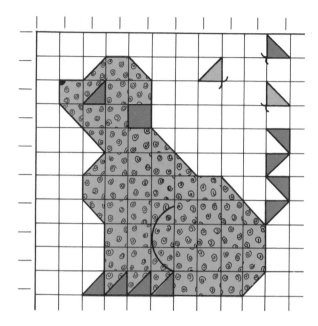

With enough patience and a wide palette of fabric colors, *any* graphed design can be adapted to piecing. Charted patterns for knitting, cross-stitch, needlepoint, and mosaic tile work offer unlimited design possibilities!

Choosing Fabrics

As for all quilts, the perfect fabric for an animal quilt will make an enormous contribution to the success of the piece. Some blocks, such as the zebra, have obvious fabric requirements (with the right black-and-white striped fabric, you can hardly miss!). Other blocks, such as the hippopotamus, may require a little research and artistic interpretation. What color is a hippo, anyway? A visit to the zoo reveals that a hippo is a dark greenish/brownish/gray, about the color of slimy algae. That doesn't sound very pleasing for a child's quilt, so a nicer shade of brown was selected for the hippo in The Zoo.

Most animals are more colorful than hippopotami, thank goodness! Do keep in mind that color is important if the animal is to be identifiable. (It would be embarrassing for your young child to say, "But Mommy, what is it?") However, if you want to make a turquoise elephant, be our guest. One of the nicest cows we've ever seen is purple.

Some animal designs will require more than one shade or print in a color to help distinguish body parts. The haunch and face on The Chocolate Rabbit were pieced in a different print (but same color) as the rest of the rabbit. This made these areas look slightly different, but they are still obviously part of the same creature. By using a print with slightly more white, these patches appear to come forward a little, giving the rabbit some dimension. It would not have been a wise choice to select dark brown for some patches and a light brown for others—it would just look odd. If you do not have two fabrics that coordinate closely, try dyeing part of the fabric in brewed tea to darken it and mellow the color.

If you find that "animal colors" are a little dull (too many grays and browns), remember that borders, backgrounds, and details can have any colors. Often, only a spark of bright color is needed to enliven your creature quilt.

Planning a Border

Many quilts, perhaps even most quilts, are enhanced by a border. But how do you know what kind to plan? Do you want to piece a design in the border or use strips of fabric as a simple frame? Your instincts will probably guide you. A busy allover design might not need a pieced border. However, a single animal block often is enhanced by a pieced border that adds to the design. The squares around a rabbit can seem to hippity hop, and the border around a panda might be a stylized version of a panda's favorite food: bamboo. On the other hand, you might want to use the animals as the border, with a traditional pattern of some kind in the quilt center.

A simple strip border does not require any special planning other than purchasing enough fabric. Simply decide how wide you want the border to be (perhaps sketching the border around the quilt design to make sure the proportion is a good one), then cut your fabric strips the correct length and width.

A pieced border requires more planning. In fact, the easiest way to plan a pieced border is to draw the border on graph paper before designing the animal. That might sound like putting the cart before the horse, but the quilt center is often more flexible than the border—especially if the border has a repeated design, such as a fence.

For some animals, you may find a traditional quilt block that would make an appropriate border. For instance, the pieced geometric design called Brown Goose could frame a goose block. Or, Kansas Troubles could frame a big, hungry grasshopper. Certainly Cats and Mice could surround a favorite pieced feline. If you don't find an appropriate border from the vast storehouse of traditional designs, just make up a new one!

Here are a few hints to help you plan a pieced border:
Often a narrow strip border between the pieced border and the quilt center will serve to frame the quilt design and keep the overall quilt design "in focus."

Pieced borders are most successful if they turn the corner in the same or similar design repeat. (If you plan your border before drafting the quilt center, this should be easy to accomplish.) Notice in the two examples that one border is more attractive than the other, even though they both use the same two pattern shapes.

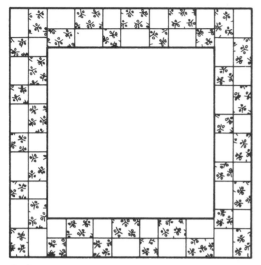

Bad

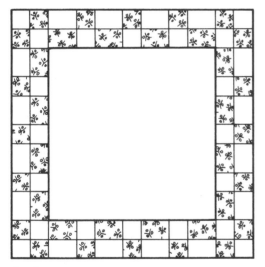

Good

The border is a good place to use fabrics that are brighter or more colorful than the animal, especially if your animal is a subdued color such as brown or gray. Be careful not to overwhelm the center, but feel free to introduce an accent color to spice up the quilt.

Remember that the binding can serve as another thin "border" if it is done in a contrasting fabric.

Although some animal patterns are intricate, with lots of angled seams that almost require hand piecing, the border often can be machine pieced. It's fine to mix techniques.

In Summary

Here is a summarized list of steps to follow in designing a pieced animal quilt:

1. Select an animal, and find several versions of the animal in books, magazines, greeting cards, or other sources. Or, draw your own. Notice the distinguishing characteristics and shapes.

2. Decide on the approximate size of the finished piece. If it is to be a bed quilt, figure out the size you'll need to allow for a pillow tuck and the "drop" on the sides of the bed. Plan on drawing a large quilt to scale on graph paper and drafting one block full size. Wall hangings up to about 40″ can be drawn full size on graph paper. Decide if you want a simple style with only a few pattern pieces, or a more realistic style.

3. Sketch your animal. Be sure it is the correct size to fill the space. Jump to Step 7 (then jump back) if you want a pieced border and you aren't sure your animal will fit the border correctly.

4. Draw the design (seam) lines. Eliminate lines that are not necessary, but retain important design characteristics.

5. Add any desired details, such as flowers, trees, eyes, and ears. These details may be appliquéd or embroidered.

6. Add seam lines in the background, making sure there is a seam line at every outside angle to allow easy piecing.

7. Plan or design the border.

8. Choose fabrics.

9. Read the next chapter.

3
Making Animal Quilts

After you have designed your animal quilt (or have chosen one of the patterns given in this book) and selected your fabrics, it's time to begin sewing. Most of the techniques used in making pieced animal quilts are identical to those used for every other kind of quilt, but we have discovered some methods that work especially well.

Making Templates

Some of the animal patterns in this book (and possibly the patterns you make) require a separate template for every piece. The easiest way to make templates is simply to trace your full-size pattern on heavy tracing paper, then cut the pieces apart. (A method for marking around paper templates is found in the next section.) Or, you can trace each pattern piece on template plastic for a stiffer template that will last through many markings. Either of these methods will yield templates without seam allowances, which are fine if you will be piecing your animal quilt by hand.

Hand piecing will probably be easier than machine piecing if your pattern has lots of angled patches or small pieces. This method allows precise stitching at a relaxed pace, although it will take you longer to complete the quilt top.

Machine piecing is great for simple patterns with fairly large patches. Angus Cows and the Scottie Quilt, for example, were both pieced by machine. If you plan on machine piecing, you will need to add seam allowances when making the templates. To do this, trace your pattern shape (these are the seam lines) and then mark additional lines outside the seam lines for the seam allowance. The typical seam allowance is ¼", which usually corresponds to the width of a sewing machine presser foot.

If the patches in your pattern are small, you might want a narrower allowance. Occasionally you may decide that wider seam allowances are called for. The Scottie Quilt was made from wool fabric, using ½" seam allowances.

It's a good idea to assign a letter or number to the upper edge of patches on your full-size pattern so you'll know which side is up. Then mark the templates to correspond. If you want to cut patches with the fabric grain line running a certain way (usually the grain lines are parallel to the edges of the block), mark each template with an arrow. Not only do these markings help you remember which template goes with which pattern and how to place patterns to get the best grain lines, they also indicate which side of the template is the right side, and which side is the reverse.

Pattern pieces that are reverses (mirror images) of other pieces will not need separate templates—the pattern template can be turned over when marking patches. *Patterns calling for reversed patches will be indicated in pattern directions by an "r" following the patch letter.*

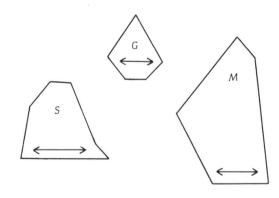

Templates for hand piecing

20

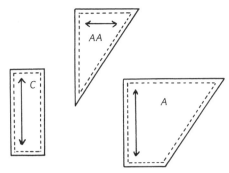

Templates for machine piecing

Marking Patches

Hand piecing requires that the seam line be accurately marked on the fabric patches, but the cutting line can be judged by eye. Place the appropriate template face down on the wrong side of the fabric, matching the grain line on the template to the grain line of the fabric, and mark around the template with a pencil. Also, lightly mark the patch letter at the upper edge. Mark the next patch, leaving about ½" between patches. (If using paper templates, place the template face down on the wrong side of the fabric, lay a ruler along the edge of the template, and mark next to the ruler.)

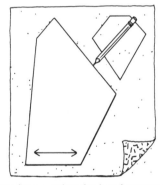

Marking patches for hand piecing

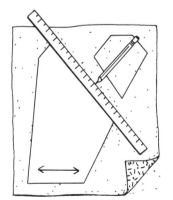

Marking around a paper template

When all the patches from a certain fabric have been marked (or when you are tired of marking), cut patches apart, leaving ¼" seam allowance outside marked lines. If your quilt block has many odd-shaped patches, it may be helpful to cut only a few at a time to keep yourself from getting confused with too many "puzzle pieces." After sewing those together, cut several more.

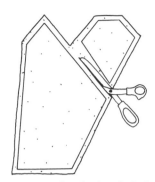

Cutting patches for hand piecing

Machine piecing requires accurate cutting lines. (When sewing, you will judge the seam line by eye with the help of your machine's presser foot or seam guide.) To mark patches for machine sewing, you can either place the appropriate template face up on the right side of the fabric and mark around the template, or you can place the template face down on the wrong side of the fabric. (If using print fabric, the pencil lines will probably show better on the wrong side of the material.) Also, mark the patch letter on the wrong side of the patch at the upper edge. It is not necessary to leave any space between marked patches. Cut patches apart on marked lines.

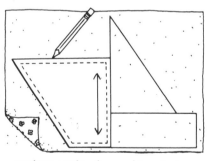

Marking patches for machine piecing

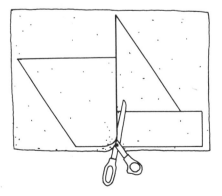

Cutting patches for machine piecing

Hand Piecing the Patches

Before beginning to sew, it is helpful to place all the patches in their correct position on a table.

As much as possible, patches should be joined in units. Small segments are joined to make larger units, then units are joined until the block is completed.

Select two adjacent patches to be joined and pin them together with right sides facing. (The seam lines will be visible.) Using thread to match the darker fabric color, sew with tiny running stitches from the beginning of the seam line (not the edge of the patch) to the end of the marked line. Begin and end each seam with a couple of backstitches.

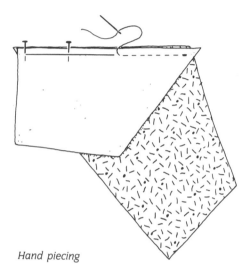

Hand piecing

Pieced animal patterns often have many angled patches, requiring setting in of corners. Hand piecing will allow precise construction of the fabric "puzzle" pieces, but how do you know in which order to join the patches for the greatest ease of assembly? Let's look at a few examples.

The four patches shown are from The Chocolate Rabbit (part of the bunny's rump and the background). There are several ways to join the patches, but one way will be better than the others.

Example #1: We could join patches S-JJ and T-KK, then join these pairs. But doesn't that look a little awkward?

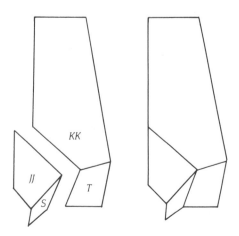

Example #2: Perhaps we could sew JJ-KK-T, then add S. It can be done, but not easily.

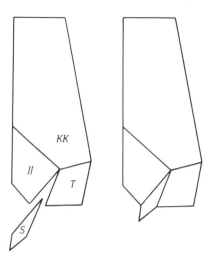

Example #3: Let's join JJ-KK, and S-T, then join these pairs. This is the best solution.

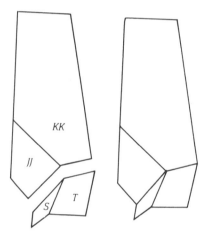

Even though it is possible to join patches in any order with hand stitching, try to avoid setting in a sharp angle.

Machine Piecing the Patches

Machine piecing will probably not be suitable for blocks with many angled patches requiring setting in of corners. Other blocks and simple borders are perfect for machine piecing, and it's almost silly not to take advantage of the sewing machine. For instance, the Scottie Quilt was easily pieced on the machine, taking only fifteen minutes to make each of the thirty-two blocks. The blocks for Grazing Cows takes even less time to make when sewn by machine.

Patches cut for machine piecing do not have marked seam lines, but must have accurate, even seam allowances. Place two adjacent patches right sides together, matching the invisible seam line by offsetting patches as necessary, and pin.

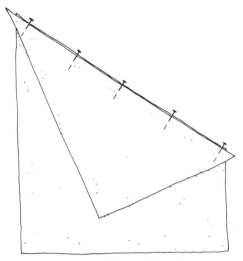

Patches pinned for machine piecing

Using thread to match the darker color fabric (or a neutral color that will not show), join the patches with short stitches, sewing from cut edge to cut edge. Use the presser foot (if it is an exact ¼") to guide your sewing to make precise ¼" seam allowances, or use the seam guide scribed on the machine throat plate.

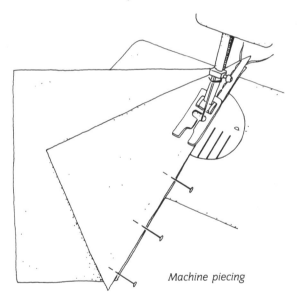

Machine piecing

Because seam allowances will be sewn down to one side or the other, you should plan in advance in which direction the allowance should fall. (Read the section in this chapter on pressing the blocks for some hints.)

Backstitching at each end of the seams is optional but will make the block less likely to come undone while handling the quilt top. It is important to backstitch when joining rows of blocks or borders, because these seams will experience some stress. Trim the thread tails as you work to avoid a tangled mess.

If you must insert an angled patch by machine, begin and end your sewing with a couple of backstitches at the exact end of the seam line (not the cut edge of the patch). If it is not easy for you to judge this placement by eye, mark the seam lines and match lines with pins when joining patches.

A Word About Curved Seams

Most of the patterns in this book use straight seams, but a few incorporate curved seams. Gentle curves can be sewn easily by machine; almost any curve can be sewn by hand. Here are a few hints:

Mark "notches" with a pencil at one or two midpoints in the seam allowances of two adjacent templates, then mark these notches on the wrong sides of the patches to be joined. When sewing, pin and sew the sections between notches (one section at a time) rather than pinning the entire seam.

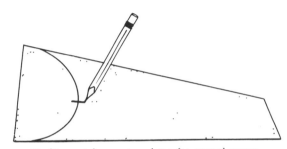

Marking notches on templates for curved seams

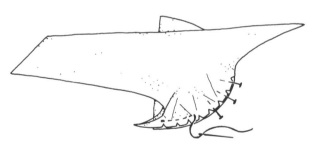

Hand piecing curved seam

Curves that dip in (concave curves) require clipping about halfway into the seam allowance. Sharp curves might require clips every ¼" or ½", and gentle curves every 2" or 3". Don't overdo the clipping—you could weaken the seam.

Curves that bulge out (convex curves) do not require clipping.

If you find the allowances too bulky after joining a curved seam, trim *one* of the allowances to about half the width.

Appliquéing the Details

Some of the design details are best done with hand appliqué. To mark patches for appliqué, use a template with no allowance added, place the template face up on the right side of the fabric, and mark around it with a pencil. Leave a scant ½" between marked patches. Cut out patches, leaving about ³⁄₁₆" turn-under allowance. Turn under the allowance just inside the marked line and baste. Position appliqués on the pieced block and blindstitch them in place, using thread to match the appliqué patch.

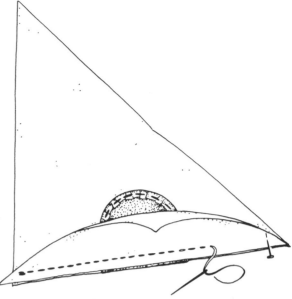

"Catching" an appliqué patch

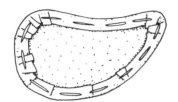

Basting turn-under allowance

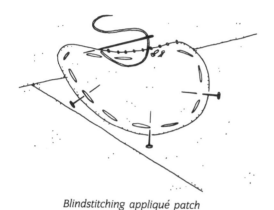

Blindstitching appliqué patch

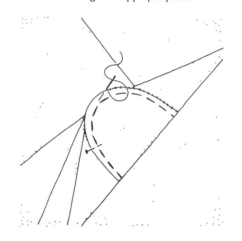

Most of the appliqué details will be added after the piecing is finished, but there are some exceptions. The ears on Panda-Panda were appliquéd, but the straight edges of these patches were caught in seams joining the forehead patches. (Often it is convenient to have one edge of an appliqué patch tucked into a seam. On the graphed and full-size patterns, a notation will tell you which edges can be "caught" in a pieced seam.)

To "catch" an appliqué, turn under and baste the allowance on all edges except the one to be caught in a pieced seam. Position this patch between the patches to be joined by piecing (being sure the patch will not be upside down after the seam is sewn) and stitch the seam. After the block has been pieced, blindstitch the appliqué in place.

If the fabric under the appliqué shows through the top patch, or if you will be quilting inside an appliqué patch, trim away the fabric behind the appliqué to leave ³⁄₁₆" allowance. If this trimming causes you to cut through a seam, finish off the seam with a few backstitches to hold it securely.

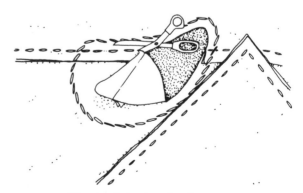

Trimming behind appliqué patch

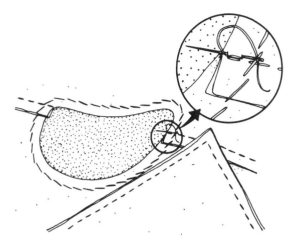

Reinforcing the cut seam

Embroidered Details

A few embroidery stitches can make a big difference in your animal quilt. A mere triangle can be transformed into a mouse with the addition of a few outline stitches and two French knots.

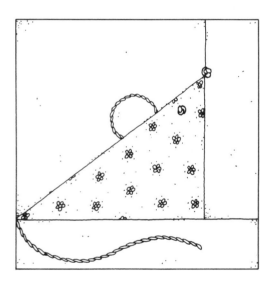

A bunny's tail can be outlined in stem stitch to make it stand out from a pale background.

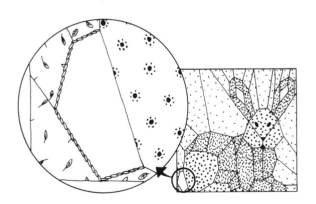

An elephant can get an eye with a few satin stitches.

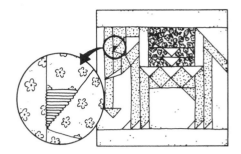

And, of course, embroidery can add your name and an inscription. Choose either embroidery floss or perle cotton and a crewel needle to add your special embroidered touches.

A Few Hints on Pressing the Blocks

Use a warm iron, with steam.

Do not press seams open (except perhaps the seam in the lining fabric, if it has been closely machine sewn).

When pressing seam allowances to one side, press so that the desired parts of the design appear to come forward. For instance, the seam allowances on the Panda-Panda's head were pressed in toward the eyes to make the face come forward slightly. To make an animal look its best, press all seam allowances around the outer edge in toward the animal.

Be careful not to stretch or scorch the block as you press it.

When pressing areas with many seam allowances, use a small sleeveboard instead of your full-size ironing board. Allow much of the block to drape over the edge of the board, exposing only the area you want to press.

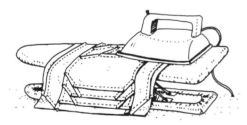

Pressing a block

Completing the Quilt

After the quilt center has been pieced, add borders. For quilts with simple strip borders, measure across the center of the quilt, both in length and width, and mark the borders (with pins) to corresponding measurements. When joining borders to the quilt top, match pins to the edges of the quilt top. Measuring through the quilt's center (rather than just sewing on strips of fabric to match the edge of the quilt top) will help you avoid rippled edges.

Lightly press the finished quilt top. Join panels of lining fabric (unless the quilt is small enough that a seam in the lining is not necessary) to make a lining 2" bigger than the quilt top all around. Assemble and baste the quilt lining, batting, and quilt top.

Many of the animal designs look best if they are quilted "in the ditch" next to seams on the sides without seam allowance. This will help the animal "puff up" slightly. If your patches are small, you need not quilt inside the animal at all. However, you can often add subtle details with quilting, such as whiskers, eyebrows, or a knothole in a tree.

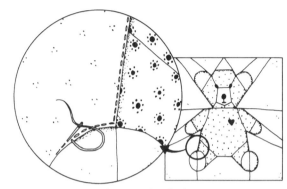

Quilting "in the ditch"

The background offers many possibilities for quilting. Simple straight or curved lines, whether in parallel lines or skew lines, will work for many designs. Again, details can be added when quilting the background. Clouds in the sky, flowers or grass, and seaweed in an aquarium are just a few ideas for quilted details.

Masking tape placed on the quilt top is terrific to help keep quilt lines straight. Most quilt shops sell ¼" masking tape, which is perfect for outline quilting ¼" from the seam. Hardware stores carry a wide variety of tape widths. Should you find that the tape leaves a small amount of sticky residue on your quilt, a dab of cleaning fluid will remove it.

The amount of quilting required depends on several factors. The first consideration is that the quilting should enhance the design of the quilt. Second, the quilting must be sufficient to hold the three layers of the quilt in place. Quilt every 2" for a cotton or wool batt, every 5" to 6" for a polyester batt, and even less if using a flannel sheet as a filler.

Bind your quilt as you would any other, using either straight-grain binding or bias, and making sure the binding is full of batting. Sew a sleeve (meaning a tube of fabric) to the back of the quilt at the top, just inside the binding, for hanging. Remember to sign and date your quilt with quilting or embroidery.

4
The Animal Alphabet

We have chosen forty-seven animals, plus a crescent moon, a rose garden, and the sun for you to play around with in planning and making quilts. These drawings are given as 4″ blocks, both out of necessity and with the idea that you can enlarge (or reduce) the patterns to suit your quilt design. Some of the block designs are easy to piece, while others will prove more challenging. Just remember: Almost any design that can be drawn on paper can be pieced in fabric. None of the block designs or project patterns in this book is any more difficult to piece than the classic Grandmother's Flower Garden pattern.

Using the Patterns

Around the edges of each 4″ block drawing you will find two sets of markings. The inside set of markings will help you enlarge patterns to make a 10″ block; the outside set will help you make a 12″ pattern. Simply decide which size block you want and use those markings to form a grid over the block drawing. Don't be shy about marking up the book (unless, of course, this copy belongs to your quilt guild or public library, in which case you'd better do a tracing first).

If you want to end up with a block in some size other than 4″, 10″, or 12″, simply make your own grid markings to correspond to the size block you need. For instance, if you want an 8″ block, divide the edges of the block drawings into eight divisions and connect your markings to complete the grid. (That was an easy one, since a 4″ block

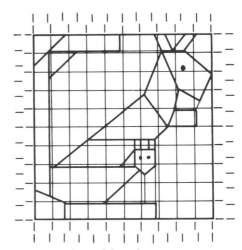

Completing the grid for enlarging

divided into eight sections means each section is ½″. Other size requirements may prove more challenging, but any size is possible!)

After you have marked your grid, enlarge the pattern square by square onto a sheet of graph paper with 1″ squares. For more advice on making enlarged patterns, see the Appendix.

One more important note: Some of the blocks, although shown as a square, are better suited to a rectangle. (The vixen is an example.) Simply take off the excess "sky" or "ground" if a rectangular animal will fit your plan better.

A Word About Scale

Something to consider when planning a quilt with animals is the size of the creature—especially how it compares with other critters in your quilt. One obvious and extreme example is the combination of elephants and mice. A quilt with equal-size blocks of elephants and mice would look pretty strange, as you can see.

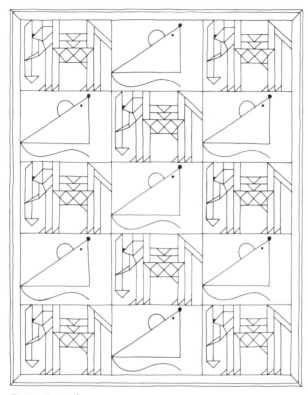

Pretty strange!

So, let's try another plan. How about a quilt of elephants with little mice as the setting squares between the sashes?

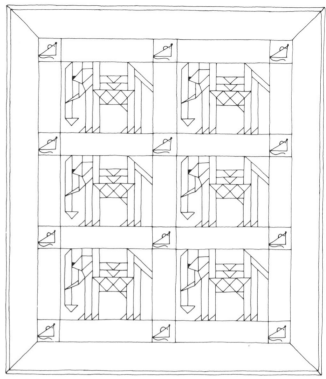

Much better!

That idea looks like it might work.

Along with each of our fifty designs, we'll give a few hints on ways to use the blocks. Enjoy the designs, and use your imagination!

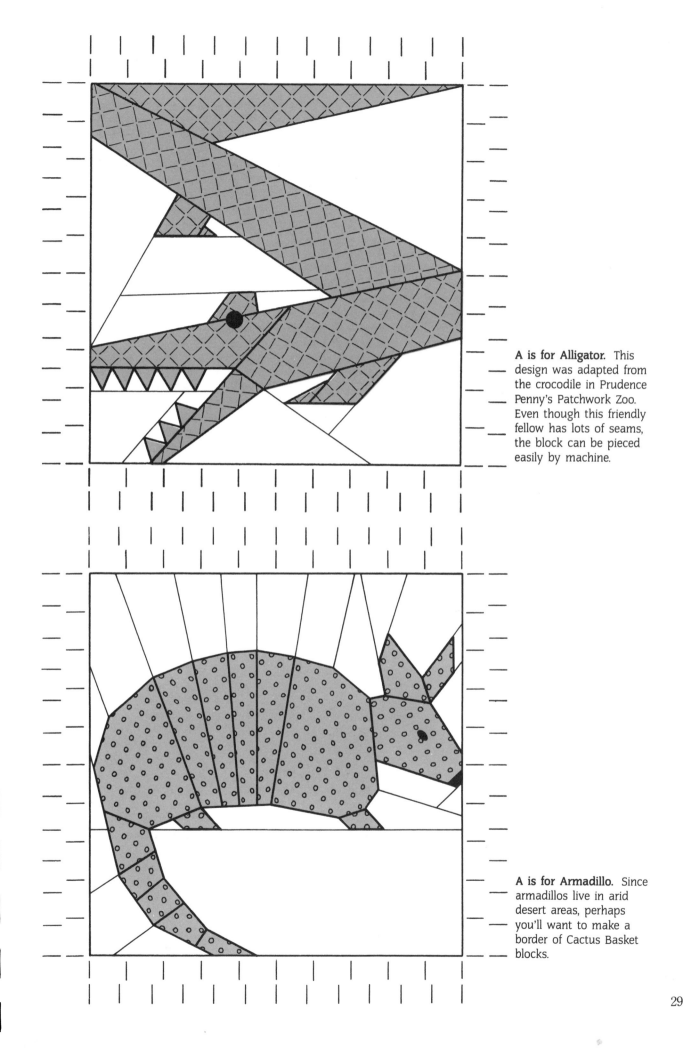

A is for Alligator. This design was adapted from the crocodile in Prudence Penny's Patchwork Zoo. Even though this friendly fellow has lots of seams, the block can be pieced easily by machine.

A is for Armadillo. Since armadillos live in arid desert areas, perhaps you'll want to make a border of Cactus Basket blocks.

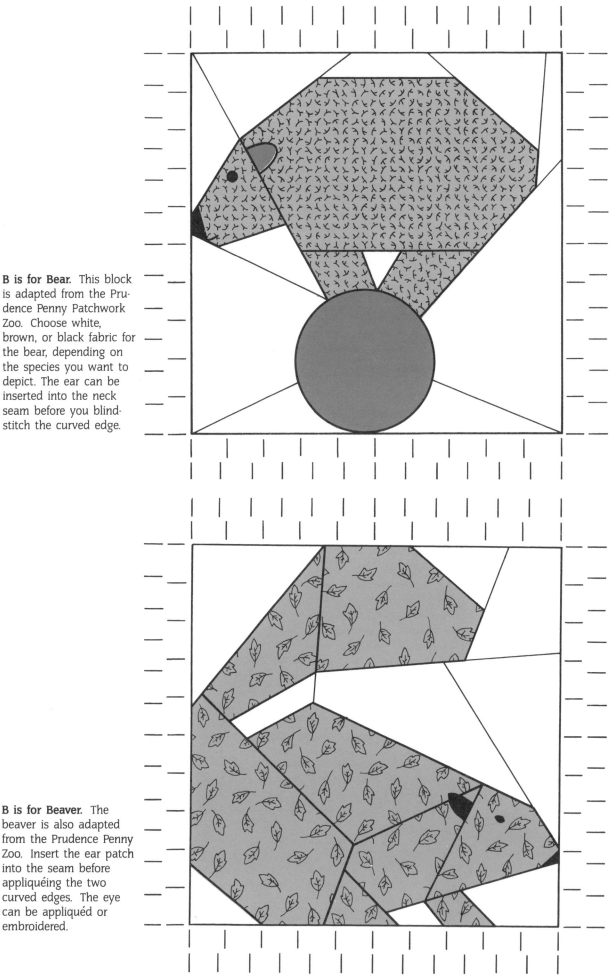

B is for Bear. This block is adapted from the Prudence Penny Patchwork Zoo. Choose white, brown, or black fabric for the bear, depending on the species you want to depict. The ear can be inserted into the neck seam before you blind-stitch the curved edge.

B is for Beaver. The beaver is also adapted from the Prudence Penny Zoo. Insert the ear patch into the seam before appliquéing the two curved edges. The eye can be appliquéd or embroidered.

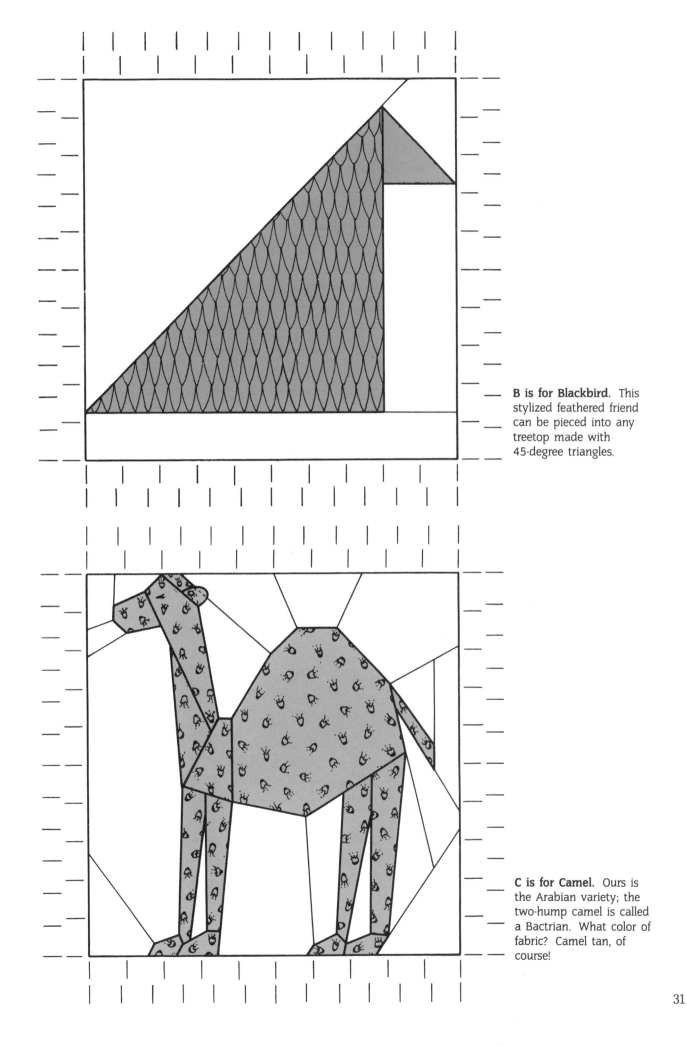

B is for Blackbird. This stylized feathered friend can be pieced into any treetop made with 45-degree triangles.

C is for Camel. Ours is the Arabian variety; the two-hump camel is called a Bactrian. What color of fabric? Camel tan, of course!

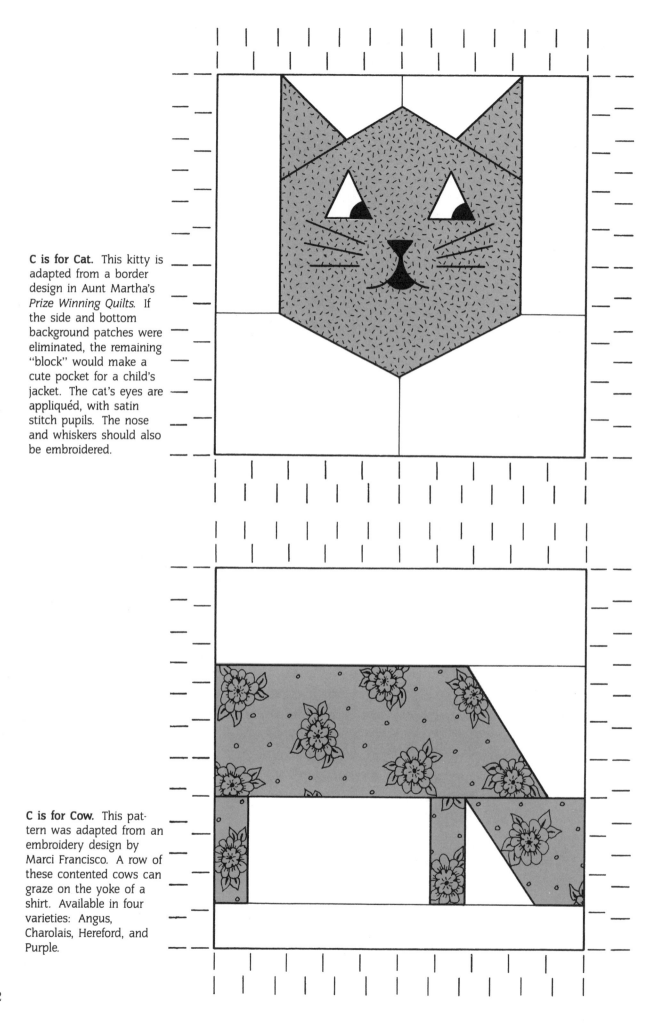

C is for Cat. This kitty is adapted from a border design in Aunt Martha's *Prize Winning Quilts.* If the side and bottom background patches were eliminated, the remaining "block" would make a cute pocket for a child's jacket. The cat's eyes are appliquéd, with satin stitch pupils. The nose and whiskers should also be embroidered.

C is for Cow. This pattern was adapted from an embroidery design by Marci Francisco. A row of these contented cows can graze on the yoke of a shirt. Available in four varieties: Angus, Charolais, Hereford, and Purple.

Horse. *Maker unknown, c. 1930. Collection of Shelly Zegart.*

Bird Patchwork. *Made by Mabel Pope Sherman Chamberlain, 1930–1935, pattern from Laura Wheeler/Alice Brooks. Collection of Betty Gustafson. Photo by Clay Kappelman.*

Ararat. *Maker unknown, c. 1931–1940, pattern appeared in* The Kansas City Star *in 1931. Collection of Linda Reuther, Julie Silber/Mary Strickler's Quilt Collection. Photo by Clay Kappelman.*

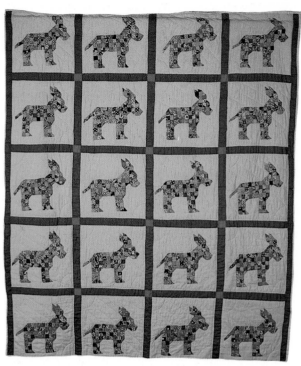

Giddap. *Maker unknown, c. 1931–1940, pattern appeared in* The Kansas City Star *in 1931. Collection of Mrs. W. A. Hudgins. Photo by Clay Kappelman. This quilt is a modification of the original pieced pattern, as the patchwork donkeys have been appliquéd to the background.*

Unnamed quilt. *Maker unknown, c. 1933. Similar quilt patterns appeared in 1928. Collection of Cathy Smith. Photo by Visual Images.*

Homarus Americanus, *©1982 by Ruth B. McDowell. 54″ × 76″. Machine piecing and quilting. Photo by David Caras.*

Brown Pelicans, ©1984 by Ruth B. McDowell. 73" × 58½". Machine piecing, hand appliqué and reverse appliqué, hand and machine quilting. Photo by David Caras.

Detail, Brown Pelicans.

Christmas Goose. *Made by Dorothy M. Brinkman.*

Counting Sheep. *Made by Barbara Brackman.*

King of Beasts. *Made by Ruth Meyer.*

Windy. *Made by Shirley C. Wedd. Shirley "painted" her beloved black labrador in this pieced portrait. As yet it is unquilted.*

Texas Treasure. *Made by Barbara Brackman. The traditional pattern "Cactus Basket" frames an armadillo.*

The Zoo. *Made by Marie Shirer. Collection of Julia Shirer.*

Angus Cows. *Made by Bonnie Reu-Hobbs.*

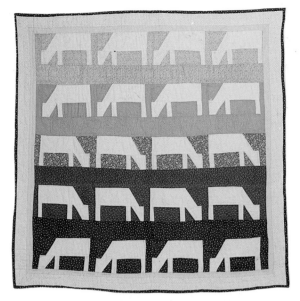

Grazing Cows: Charolais. *Made by Barbara Brackman.*

Kansas Herefords. *Made by Jeanette Dickson.*

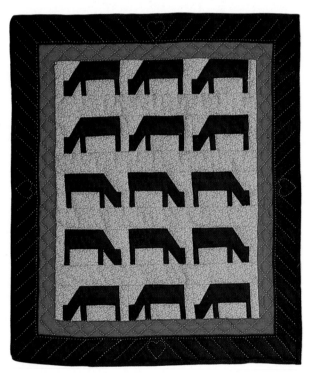

Teeny-Moos. *Doll quilt, made by Bonnie Reu-Hobbs.*

Stormstown Cows. *Made by Rebecca Shirer. Photo by Nels Shirer.*

Detail, Stormstown Cows.

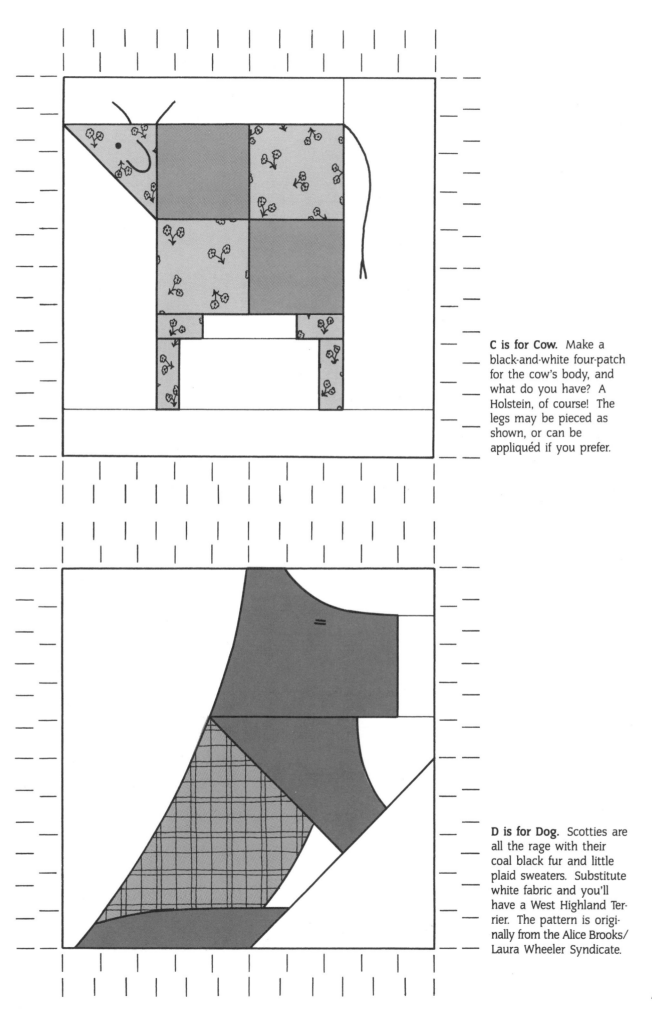

C is for Cow. Make a black-and-white four-patch for the cow's body, and what do you have? A Holstein, of course! The legs may be pieced as shown, or can be appliquéd if you prefer.

D is for Dog. Scotties are all the rage with their coal black fur and little plaid sweaters. Substitute white fabric and you'll have a West Highland Terrier. The pattern is originally from the Alice Brooks/Laura Wheeler Syndicate.

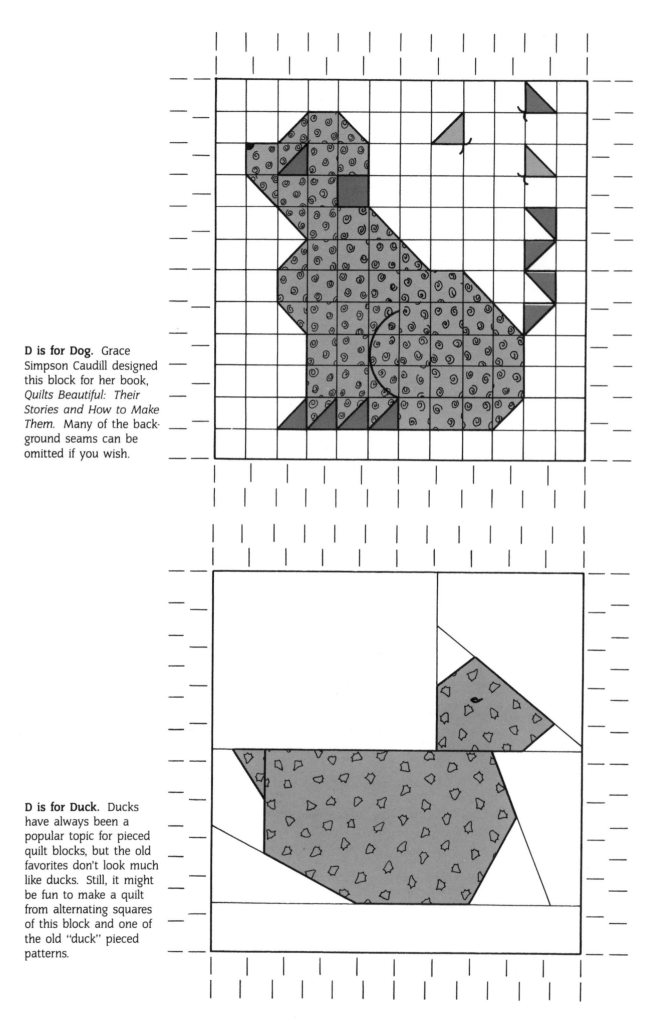

D is for Dog. Grace Simpson Caudill designed this block for her book, *Quilts Beautiful: Their Stories and How to Make Them.* Many of the background seams can be omitted if you wish.

D is for Duck. Ducks have always been a popular topic for pieced quilt blocks, but the old favorites don't look much like ducks. Still, it might be fun to make a quilt from alternating squares of this block and one of the old "duck" pieced patterns.

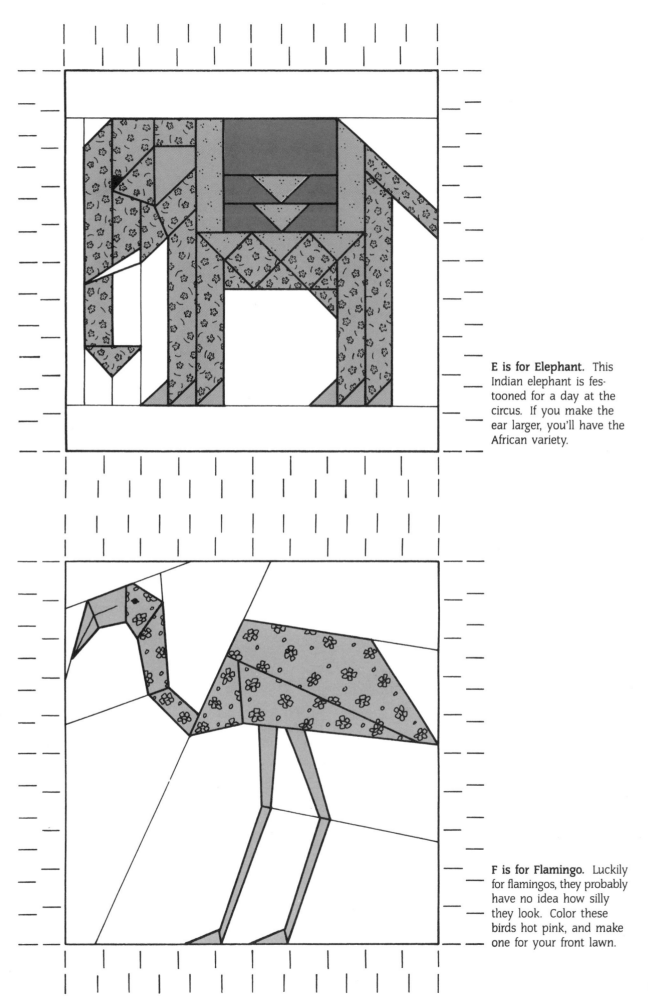

E is for Elephant. This Indian elephant is festooned for a day at the circus. If you make the ear larger, you'll have the African variety.

F is for Flamingo. Luckily for flamingos, they probably have no idea how silly they look. Color these birds hot pink, and make one for your front lawn.

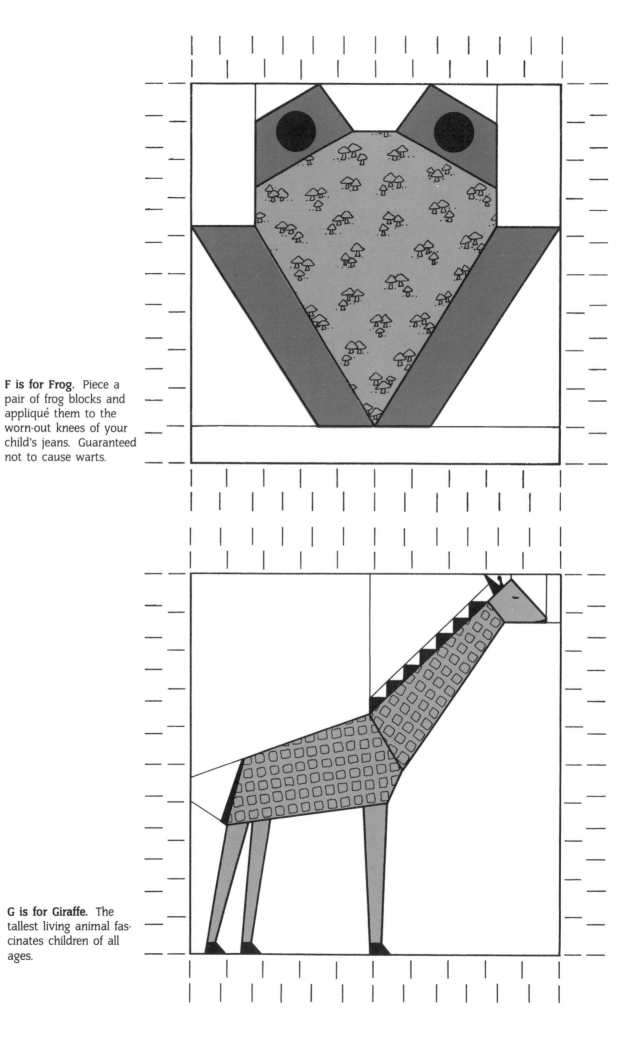

F is for Frog. Piece a pair of frog blocks and appliqué them to the worn-out knees of your child's jeans. Guaranteed not to cause warts.

G is for Giraffe. The tallest living animal fascinates children of all ages.

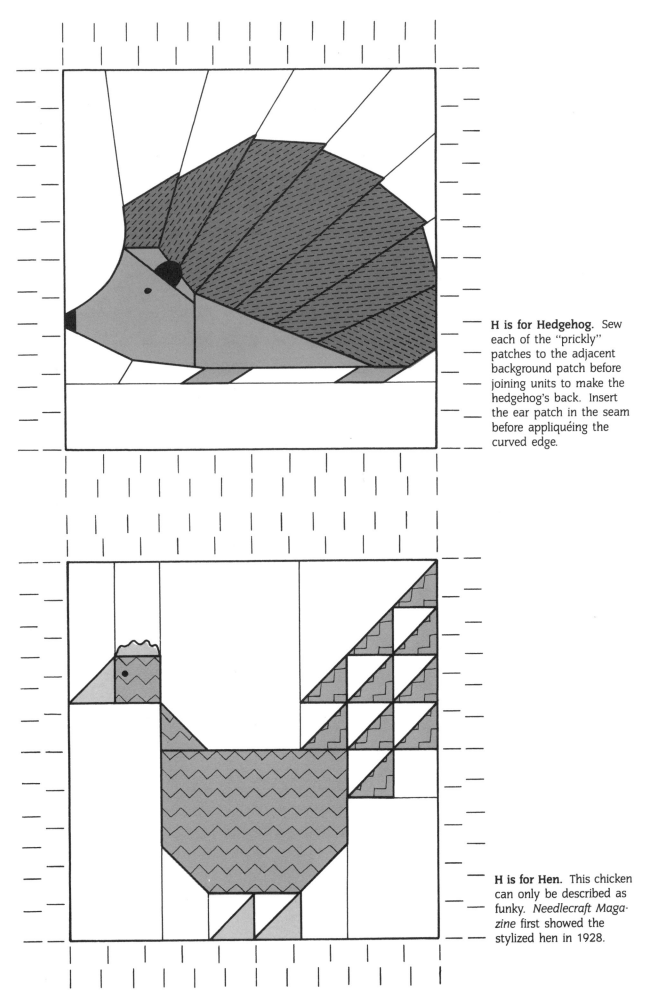

H is for Hedgehog. Sew each of the "prickly" patches to the adjacent background patch before joining units to make the hedgehog's back. Insert the ear patch in the seam before appliquéing the curved edge.

H is for Hen. This chicken can only be described as funky. *Needlecraft Magazine* first showed the stylized hen in 1928.

45

H is for Hippopotamus.
Prudence Penny included
a pieced hippo in the
1933 zoo, but the original
instructions called for
appliquéing the animal to
a background block. In
our version, only the
teeth and ear are
appliquéd (after inserting
the straight edges in
seams). The eye can be
embroidered.

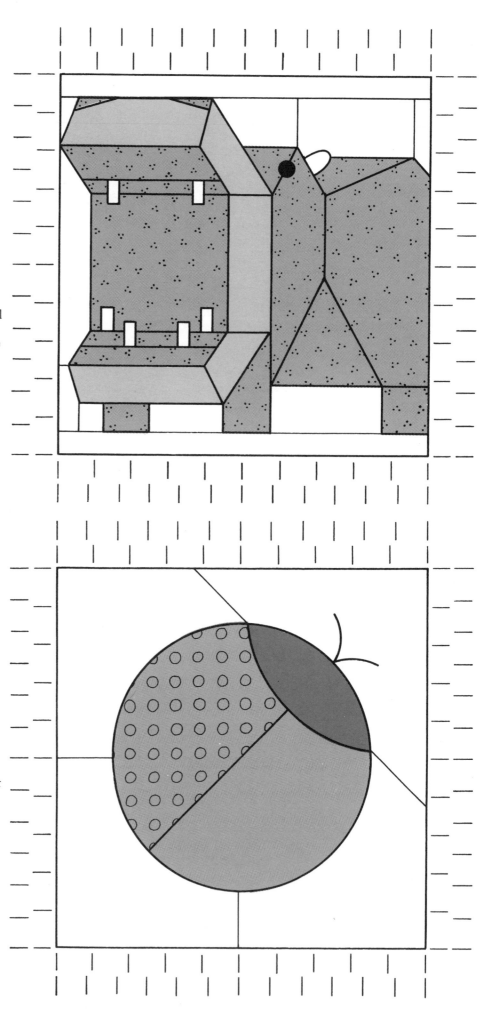

I is for Insect. A similar
ladybug first appeared in
a May 1966 issue of *Aunt
Kate's Quilting Bee*. The
piecing will be easy if
you mark notches on the
curved edges of adjacent
templates. After marking
these notches in the
patch seam allowances,
hand-stitch from notch to
notch for perfect piecing.
Embroider the antennae
in outline stitch.

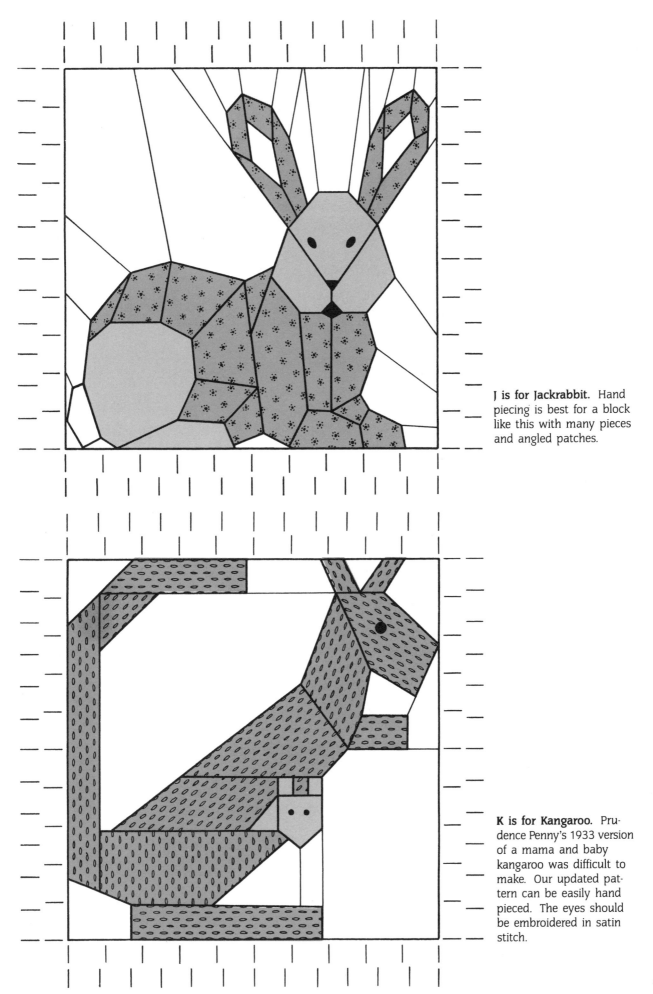

J is for Jackrabbit. Hand piecing is best for a block like this with many pieces and angled patches.

K is for Kangaroo. Prudence Penny's 1933 version of a mama and baby kangaroo was difficult to make. Our updated pattern can be easily hand pieced. The eyes should be embroidered in satin stitch.

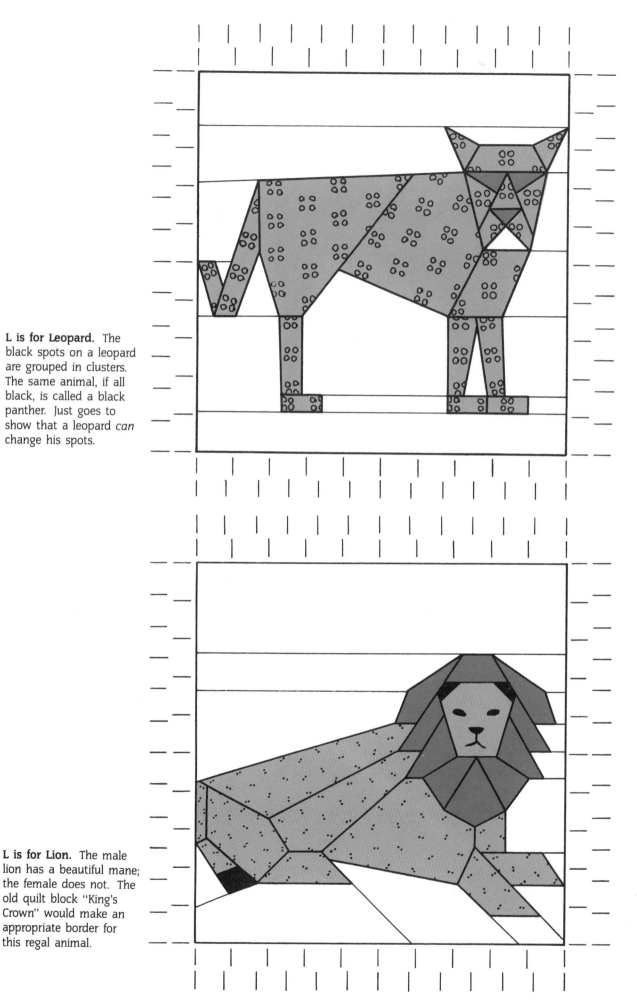

L is for Leopard. The black spots on a leopard are grouped in clusters. The same animal, if all black, is called a black panther. Just goes to show that a leopard *can* change his spots.

L is for Lion. The male lion has a beautiful mane; the female does not. The old quilt block "King's Crown" would make an appropriate border for this regal animal.

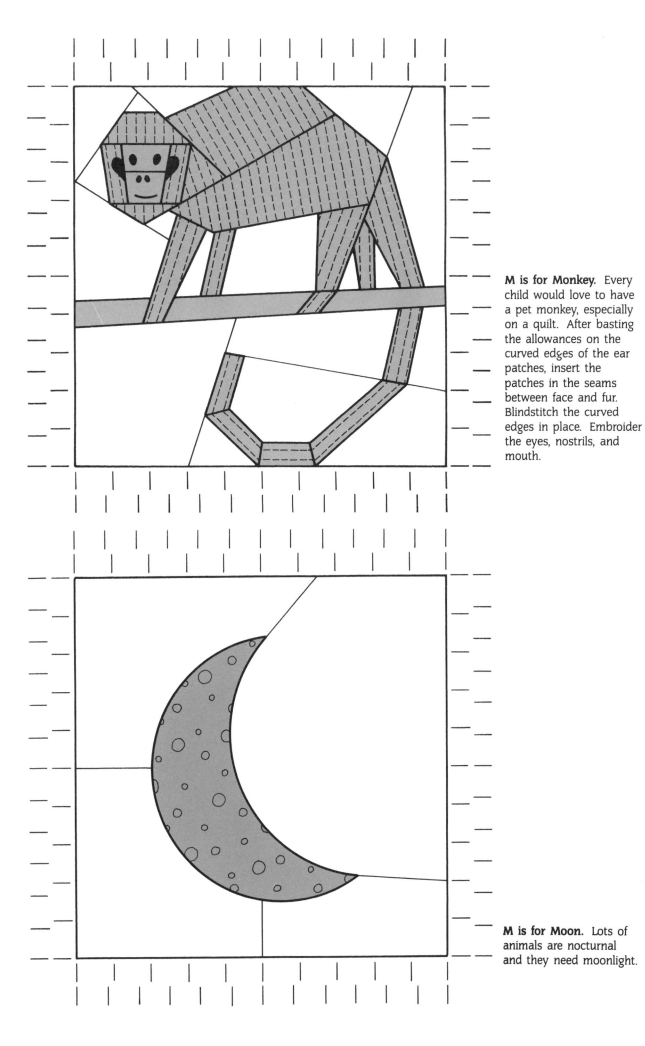

M is for Monkey. Every child would love to have a pet monkey, especially on a quilt. After basting the allowances on the curved edges of the ear patches, insert the patches in the seams between face and fur. Blindstitch the curved edges in place. Embroider the eyes, nostrils, and mouth.

M is for Moon. Lots of animals are nocturnal and they need moonlight.

49

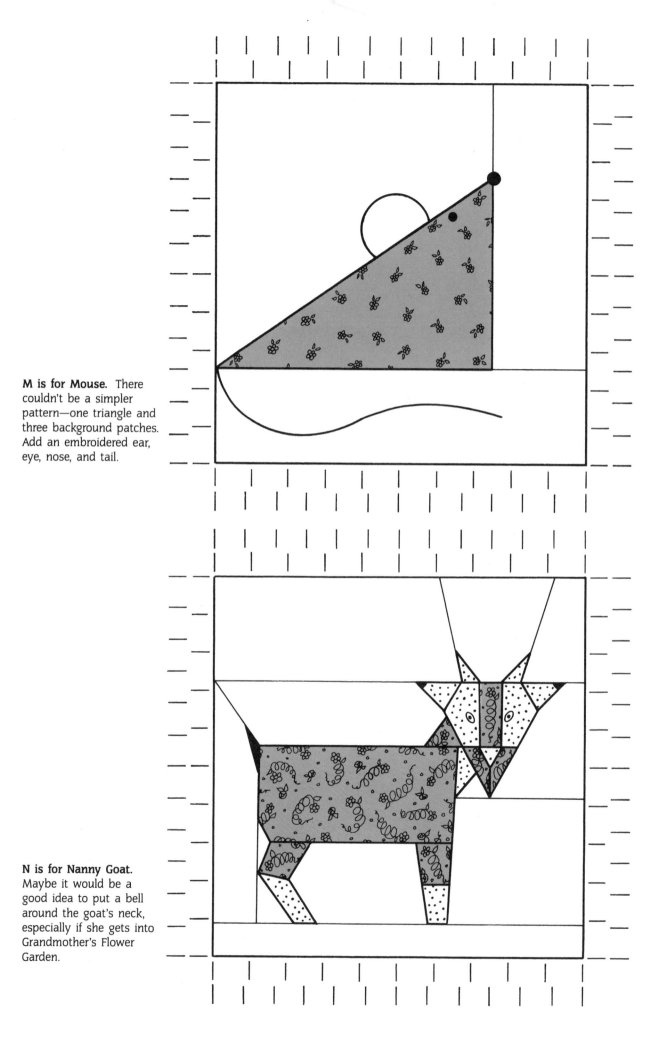

M is for Mouse. There couldn't be a simpler pattern—one triangle and three background patches. Add an embroidered ear, eye, nose, and tail.

N is for Nanny Goat. Maybe it would be a good idea to put a bell around the goat's neck, especially if she gets into Grandmother's Flower Garden.

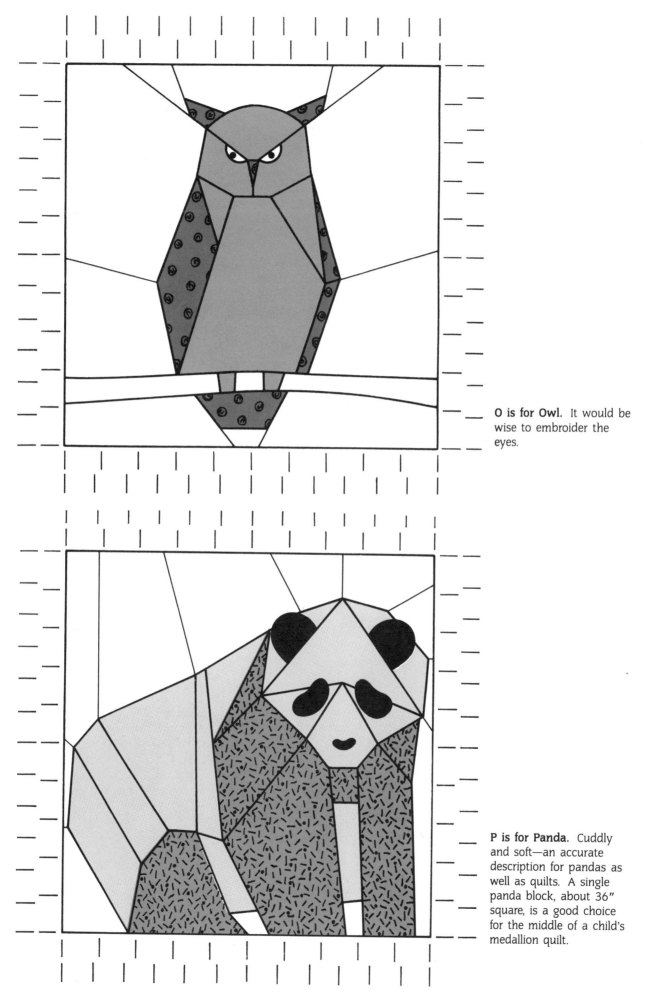

O is for Owl. It would be wise to embroider the eyes.

P is for Panda. Cuddly and soft—an accurate description for pandas as well as quilts. A single panda block, about 36″ square, is a good choice for the middle of a child's medallion quilt.

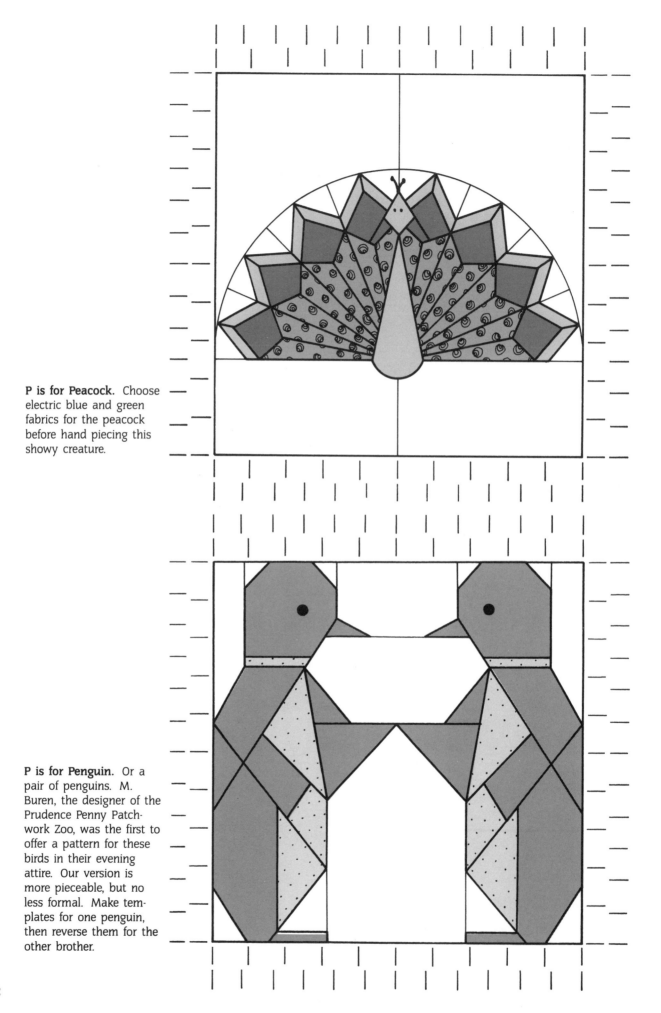

P is for Peacock. Choose electric blue and green fabrics for the peacock before hand piecing this showy creature.

P is for Penguin. Or a pair of penguins. M. Buren, the designer of the Prudence Penny Patchwork Zoo, was the first to offer a pattern for these birds in their evening attire. Our version is more pieceable, but no less formal. Make templates for one penguin, then reverse them for the other brother.

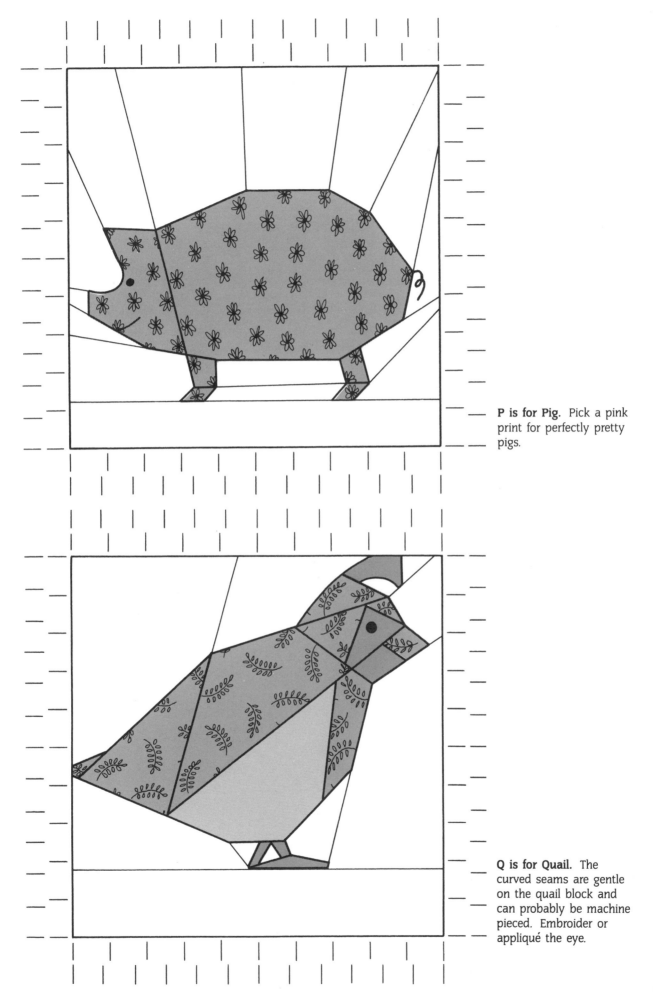

P is for Pig. Pick a pink print for perfectly pretty pigs.

Q is for Quail. The curved seams are gentle on the quail block and can probably be machine pieced. Embroider or appliqué the eye.

53

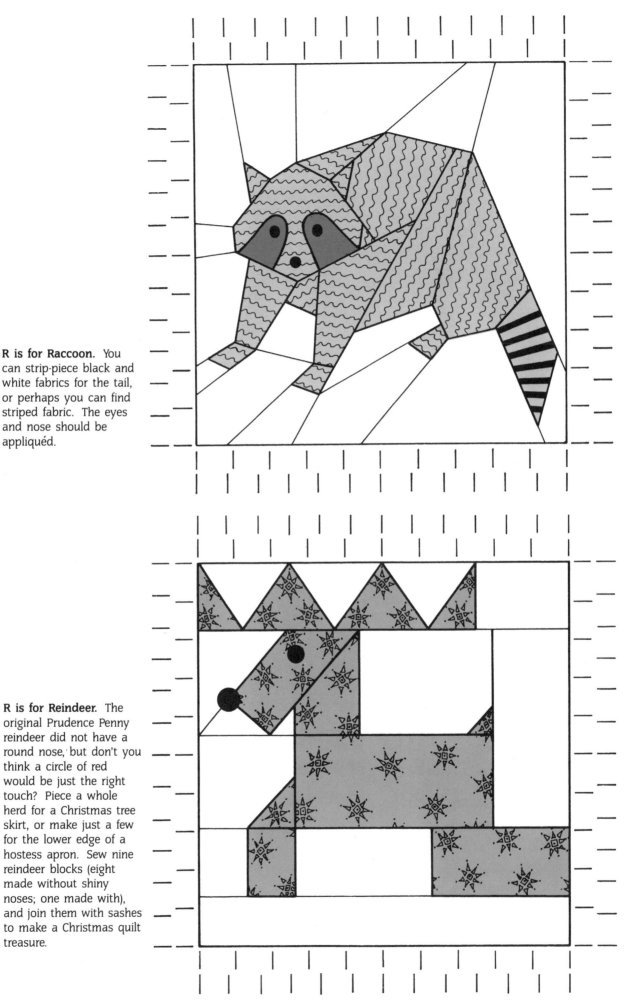

R is for Raccoon. You can strip-piece black and white fabrics for the tail, or perhaps you can find striped fabric. The eyes and nose should be appliquéd.

R is for Reindeer. The original Prudence Penny reindeer did not have a round nose, but don't you think a circle of red would be just the right touch? Piece a whole herd for a Christmas tree skirt, or make just a few for the lower edge of a hostess apron. Sew nine reindeer blocks (eight made without shiny noses; one made with), and join them with sashes to make a Christmas quilt treasure.

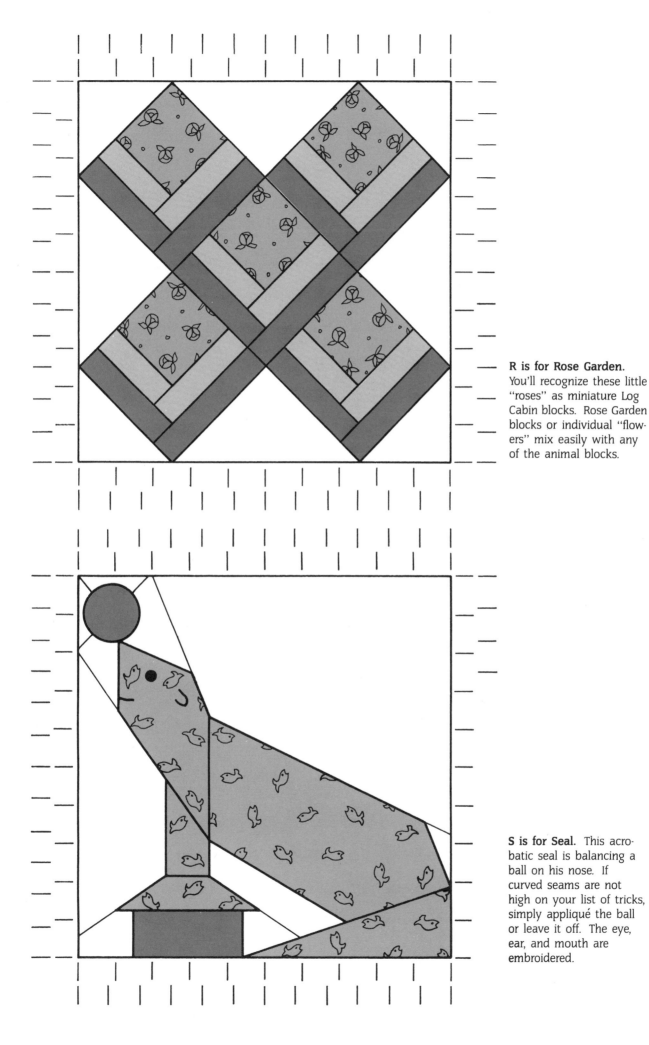

R is for Rose Garden.
You'll recognize these little "roses" as miniature Log Cabin blocks. Rose Garden blocks or individual "flowers" mix easily with any of the animal blocks.

S is for Seal. This acrobatic seal is balancing a ball on his nose. If curved seams are not high on your list of tricks, simply appliqué the ball or leave it off. The eye, ear, and mouth are embroidered.

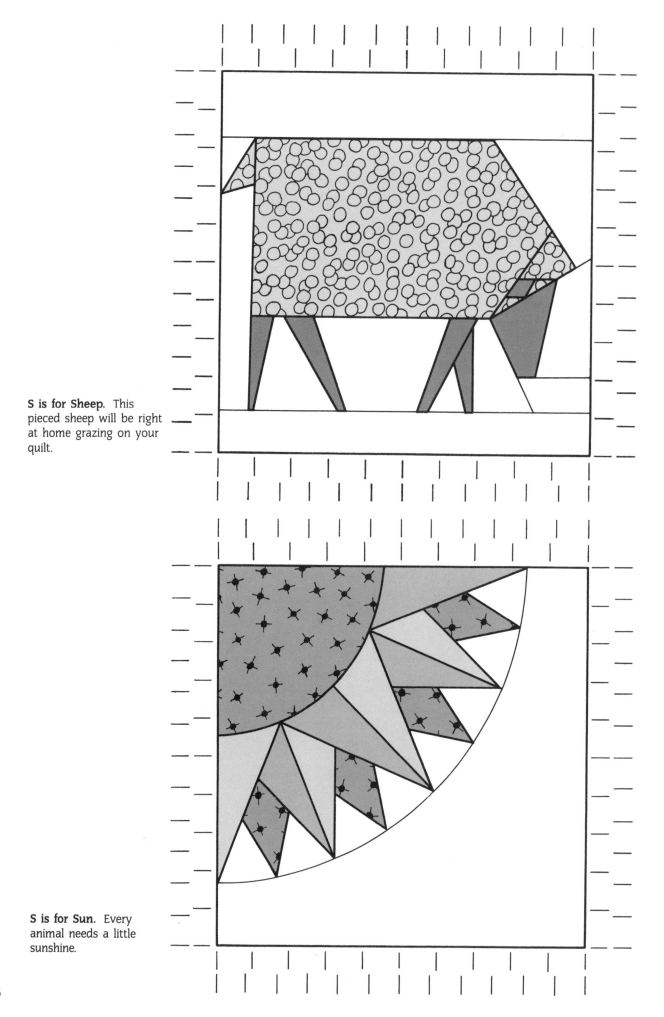

S is for Sheep. This pieced sheep will be right at home grazing on your quilt.

S is for Sun. Every animal needs a little sunshine.

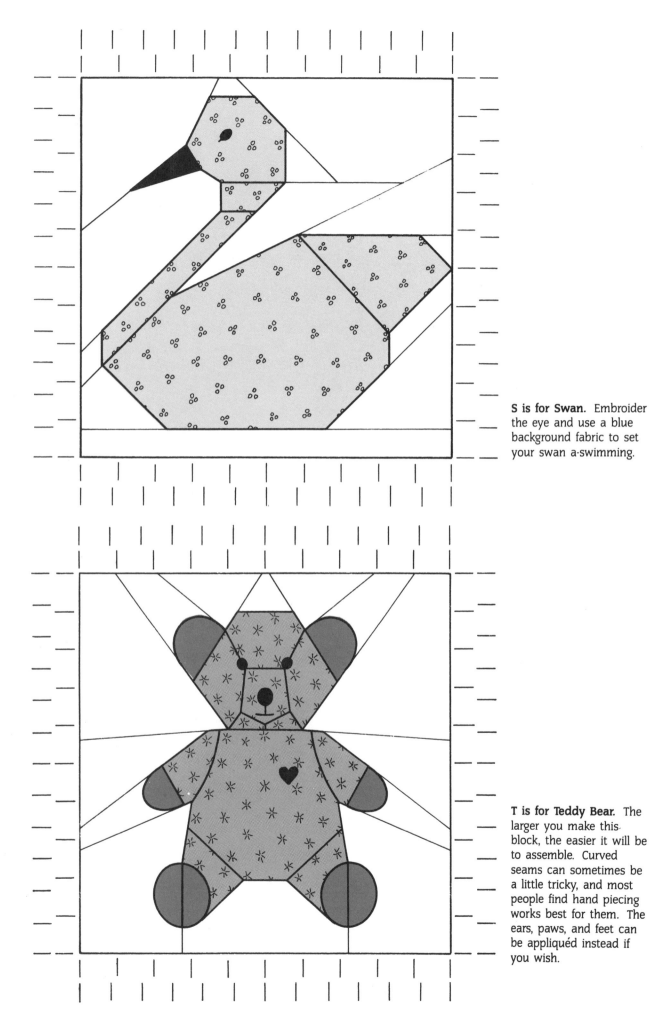

S is for Swan. Embroider the eye and use a blue background fabric to set your swan a-swimming.

T is for Teddy Bear. The larger you make this block, the easier it will be to assemble. Curved seams can sometimes be a little tricky, and most people find hand piecing works best for them. The ears, paws, and feet can be appliquéd instead if you wish.

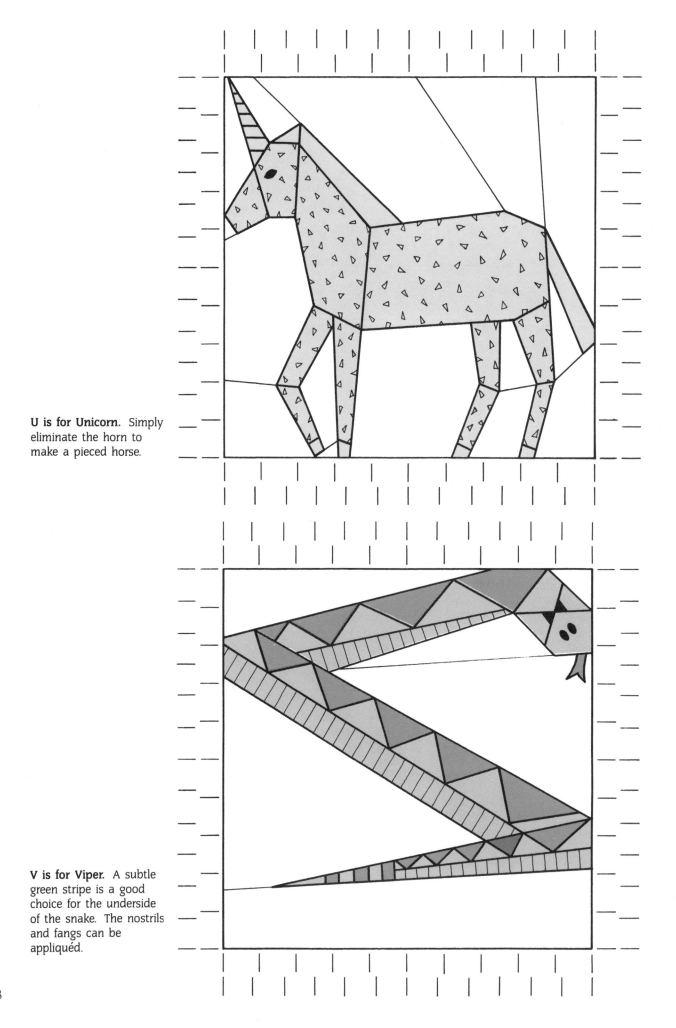

U is for Unicorn. Simply eliminate the horn to make a pieced horse.

V is for Viper. A subtle green stripe is a good choice for the underside of the snake. The nostrils and fangs can be appliquéd.

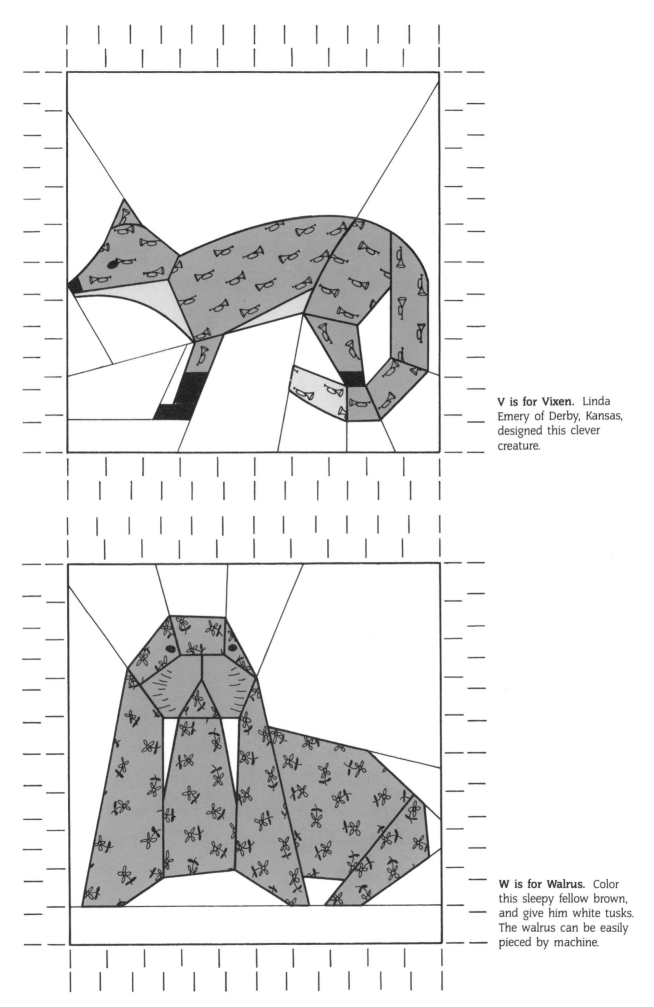

V is for Vixen. Linda Emery of Derby, Kansas, designed this clever creature.

W is for Walrus. Color this sleepy fellow brown, and give him white tusks. The walrus can be easily pieced by machine.

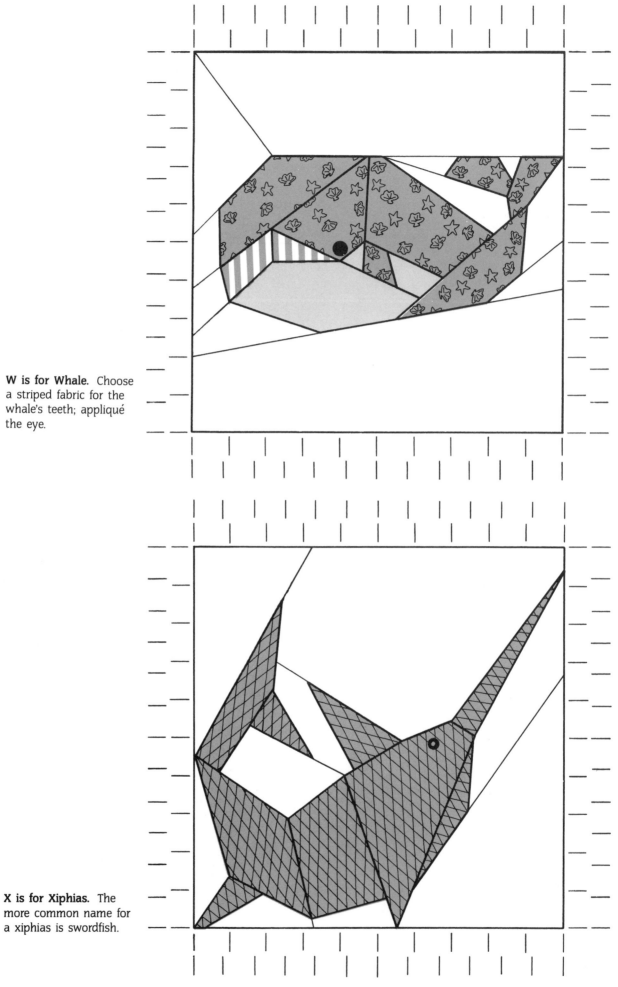

W is for Whale. Choose a striped fabric for the whale's teeth; appliqué the eye.

X is for Xiphias. The more common name for a xiphias is swordfish.

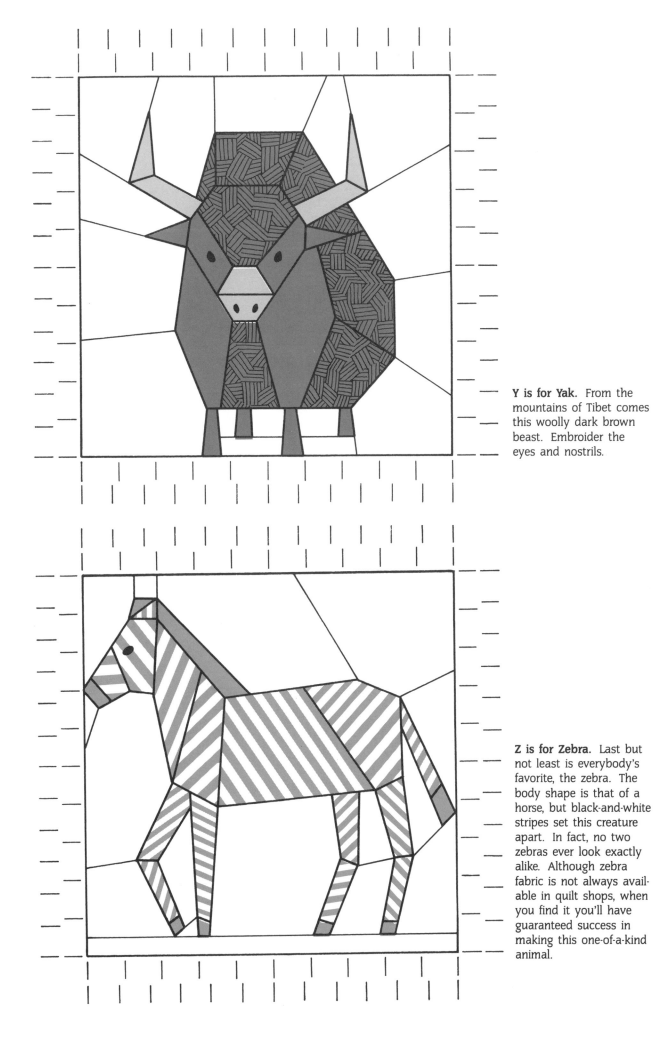

Y is for Yak. From the mountains of Tibet comes this woolly dark brown beast. Embroider the eyes and nostrils.

Z is for Zebra. Last but not least is everybody's favorite, the zebra. The body shape is that of a horse, but black-and-white stripes set this creature apart. In fact, no two zebras ever look exactly alike. Although zebra fabric is not always available in quilt shops, when you find it you'll have guaranteed success in making this one-of-a-kind animal.

5
The Animal Projects

Animal Alphabet Quilt

Quilt Size: 60½″ × 98″ for a twin bed.

Yardage (44″ fabric) and Cutting Requirements

Fabric A . . . . 2⅞ yards
  Two borders 4½″ × 98½″, two borders 4½″ × 61″, binding 1½″ × 9⅜ yards, fourteen A, fourteen Ar
Fabric B . . . . 1⅝ yards
  67 sashes 3″ × 10½″
Fabric C . . . . ⅜ yard
  Twenty-six setting squares 3″ × 3″, fourteen B, fourteen Br, fourteen C, fourteen Cr
Prints and solids . . . . as needed
  Patches for twenty-eight quilt blocks (one block for each letter of the alphabet, plus two other blocks of your choice)
Lining fabric . . . . 5⅞ yards
Batting . . . . 64½″ × 102″

Assembly Instructions

Choose one animal block for each letter of the alphabet, plus two other blocks of your choice. Enlarge patterns, or draft your own, to finish 10″ square. Make twenty-eight blocks.

Fourteen of the setting squares are pieced hearts made from A, B, and C patches. Join patches to make fourteen heart setting squares. The remaining setting squares are made by embroidering 2″ alphabet letters on 3″ × 3″ patches. (Use stencil lettering, or draw simple block letters.)

Embroider twenty-eight sashes as shown in quilt drawing. (Lettering can be hand-written or traced from an alphabet book.)

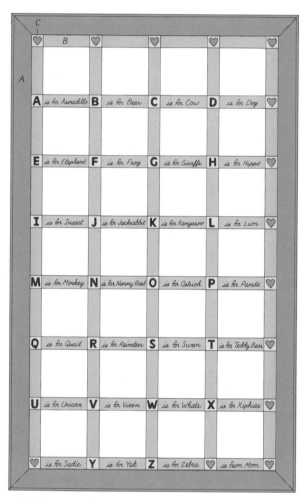

Add ¼″ seam allowances to patches for animal blocks and patches A, B, and C.

Join setting squares, sashes, and blocks in horizontal rows. The top row will have five heart setting squares sewn alternately with four plain sashes. Row 2 will have the A, B, C, and D blocks joined alternately with five plain sashes. Row 3 will have the A, B, C, and D setting squares and a heart setting square joined with the A, B, C, and D embroidered sashes. Rows 4-15 are made similarly. Join rows in correct order.

Sew short borders to top and bottom of quilt. Sew long borders to sides of quilt. Miter corners, trimming excess to leave ¼" seam allowances.

Lightly press the quilt top, pressing sash seam allowances away from quilt blocks.

Assemble and baste quilt lining, batting, and quilt top. Quilt "in the ditch" next to each animal, heart, and sash. Quilt background and border as desired.

Finish the quilt with binding.

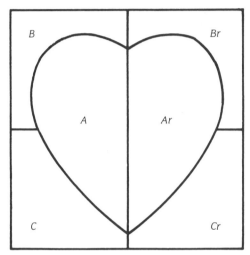

Heart Setting Square

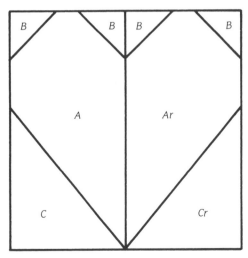

Optional Heart Setting Square

Dinosaur

Size: 18" hoop hanging.

Yardage (44" fabric) and Cutting Requirements

Black print . . . . ⅛ yard
    Four J, one O, one P, five Q
Brown print . . . . ¼ yard
    One each A, B, C, D, E, F, G, H, I, K, L, M, N
Green print . . . . ¼ yard
    One II, one IIr, three JJ, one KK, one LL, one MM, one QQ, one RR, one TT
Blue solid . . . . ¼ yard
    One AA, one BB, one CC, one CCr, one DD, one EE, five FF, one GG, one HH, one NN, one OO, one PP, one SS, one UU
Lining fabric . . . . 24" × 24"
Batting . . . . 24" × 24"
Notions: black embroidery floss, 18" quilt hoop, black spray paint, 2½ yards bias tape, 2 yards cording

Assembly Instructions

Join patches by hand as indicated in drawing to complete the block.

Using black floss, embroider nostril and eye in lazy daisy stitch, adding extra straight stitches at corners of eye. Embroider mouth in backstitch.

Press seam allowances around edge of dinosaur toward the animal.

Assemble and baste quilt lining, batting, and pieced top. Outline-quilt ¼" outside dinosaur.

Lazy Daisy Stitch

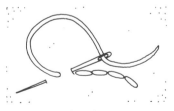

Backstitch

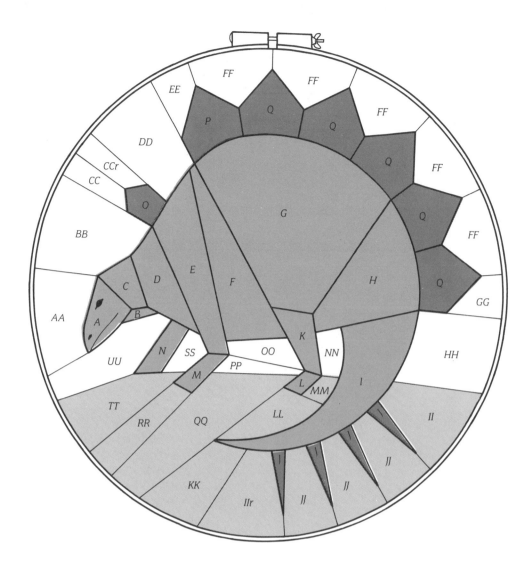

Machine sew bias tape around the edge of the quilted circle, placing right side of bias tape next to quilt top. Fold bias tape to the back and stitch again to form a casing, leaving 2″ open. Run cording through the casing.

Lightly sand hoop if it has a wax finish. Spray paint hoop black. (Paint must be thoroughly dry before you mount quilt block.)

Mount quilt block in hoop and tighten wing nut on hoop. Pull cording tight, and tie ends securely.

Dinosaur. *Made by Marie Shirer. Collection of Daniel Shirer.*

Garden of Eden. *Made by Barbara Brackman.*

Noah's Ark. *Blocks designed and quilt made by Linda Emery from a quilt design by Barbara Brackman.*

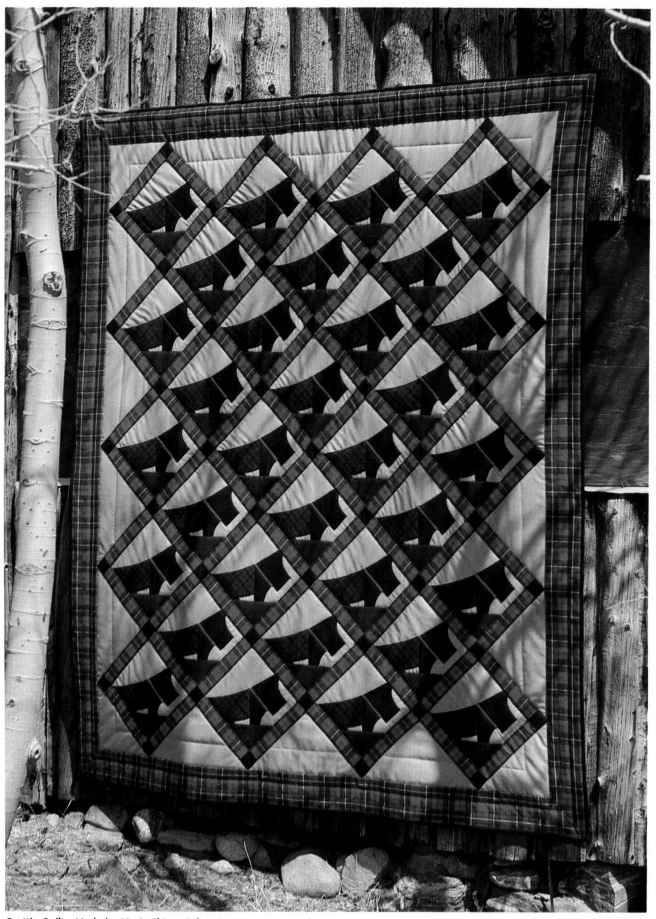

Scottie Quilt. *Made by Marie Shirer. Fabric is 100 percent wool.*

Sit Up and Beg. *Pillow, made by Marie Shirer.*

Teddy Bear. *Made by Linda Emery from a design by Marie Shirer.*

The Chocolate Rabbit. *Made by Marie Shirer. Collection of Jessica Bender.*

Rasperries for Supper. *Made by Mary Ann Johnson from a design by Marie Shirer.*

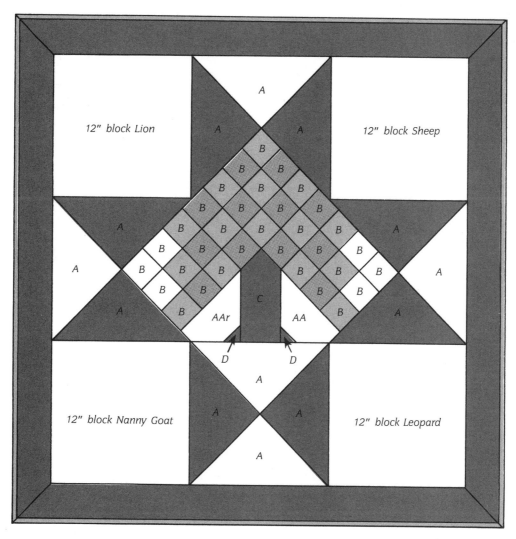

Garden of Eden is shown on page 66.

Garden of Eden

Quilt Size: 42″ × 42″ for a wall hanging.

Yardage (44″ fabric) and Cutting Requirements

Dark green stripe . . . . 1¼ yards
   Four borders 3½″ × 42½″, eight A, one C, two D
Medium green print . . . . ½ yard
   Binding 1½″ × 5⅛ yards, fifteen B
Red print . . . . ⅛ yard
   Twelve B
Beige print . . . . 1 yard
   Five A, one AA, one AAr, six B, and background patches
   for four 12″ animal blocks
Various fabrics . . . . scraps
   Patches for four 12″ animal blocks (lion, sheep, nanny
   goat, and leopard, or others of your choice)
Lining fabric . . . . 2⅝ yards
Batting . . . . 46″ × 46″

Assembly Instructions

Enlarge patterns (or draft your own) for lion, sheep, nanny goat, and leopard, or others of your choice, to finish 12″ squares. Using beige print fabric in background patches, complete four animal blocks.

Make center Tree of Temptation block using B, C, D, AA, and AAr patches; sew beige print A to bottom. Sew dark green stripe A's to the top and right-hand edges of the nanny goat block, to the top and left-hand edges of the leopard block, to the bottom and left-hand edges of the sheep block, and to the bottom and right-hand edges of the lion block. Join the five blocks and remaining beige print A's to complete quilt center.

Add borders, mitering corners and trimming excess.

Assemble and baste quilt lining, batting, and quilt top. Quilt background in parallel lines approximately 1″ apart. Quilt "in the ditch" around all animal patches and next to border.

Finish the quilt with medium green print binding.

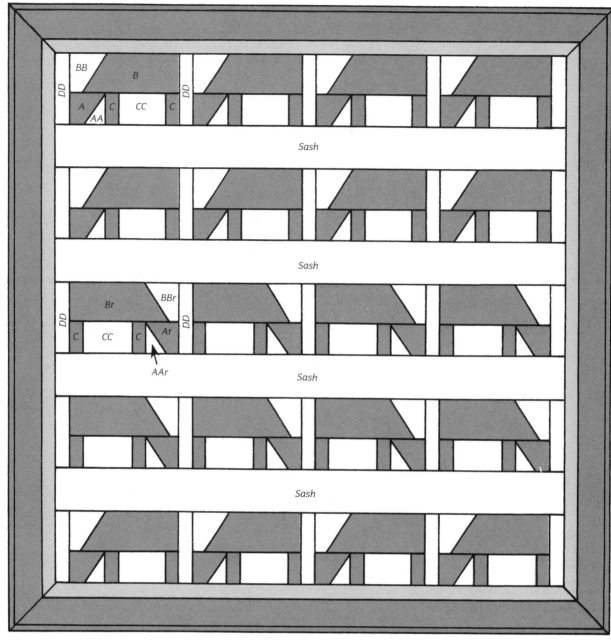

Grazing Cows quilt is shown on page 39.

Grazing Cows

Quilt Size: 43" × 43" for a wall hanging or child's quilt.

Yardage (44" fabric) and Cutting Requirements

Note: Fabric requirements are listed for Charolais (white) cows. Substitute fabrics for Hereford (reddish-brown) and Angus (black) cows as you wish.

White solid . . . . .1⅜ yards
   Four border strips 2½" × 43½", twelve A, eight Ar, twelve
   B, eight Br, forty C

Pink solid . . . . .¼ yard
   Four border strips 1½" × 39½"

Very dark green print .1¼ yards
   Binding 1½" × 5⅜ yards, one sash 3½" × 37½", four AA,
   four BB, four CC, five DD

Dark green print . . . . .⅜ yard
   One sash 3½" × 37½", four AAr, four BBr, four CC, five DD

Medium green print . . . . .¼ yard
   Four AAr, four BBr, four CC, five DD

Light green print . . . . .⅜ yard
   One sash 3½" × 37½", four AA, four BB, four CC, five DD

Very light green print . . . . .⅜ yard
   One sash 3½" × 37½", four AA, four BB, four CC, five DD

Lining fabric . . . . .2¾ yards

Batting . . . . .47" × 47"

Sash and border dimensions include seam allowances.

Assembly Instructions

    As shown in quilt drawing, cows in rows 1, 2, and 5 face to the left, and cows in rows 3 and 4 face to the right. Make four cow blocks for each row, using the same print fabric in the background for all cows in one row. Join four cow blocks alternately with five DD patches, matching fabric in DD's to background fabrics in cow blocks.

Join rows of cows and sashes (working from top of quilt) in this order: very light green row, very light green sash, light green row, light green sash, medium green row, dark green sash, dark green row, very dark green sash, very dark green row.

Add pink borders, then white borders, mitering corners and trimming excess to leave ¼" seam allowances.

Lightly press the quilt top, pressing seam allowances on cow rows toward the cows.

Using a pencil or water-erasable marking pen, lightly mark the word "cow" in the sashes above each pieced cow.

Assemble and baste quilt lining, batting, and quilt top. Quilt "in the ditch" around each cow and next to each border strip. Quilt as marked.

Finish the quilt with very dark green binding.

Noah's Ark

Quilt Size: 42" × 42" for a child's quilt or wall hanging.

Yardage (44" fabric) and Cutting Requirements

Sky blue solid . . . . .¼ yard
   One each AA, AAr, BB, BBr, CC, DD, EE, FF, GG, HH, II (for sky)
Light blue solid . . . . .¼ yard
   One A (for ocean)
Medium blue print . . . . .1¼ yards
   Four borders 3½" × 42½"
Gold/brown stripe . . . . .⅝ yard
   Eight A
Dark brown solid . . . . .¼ yard
   One B, olive branch

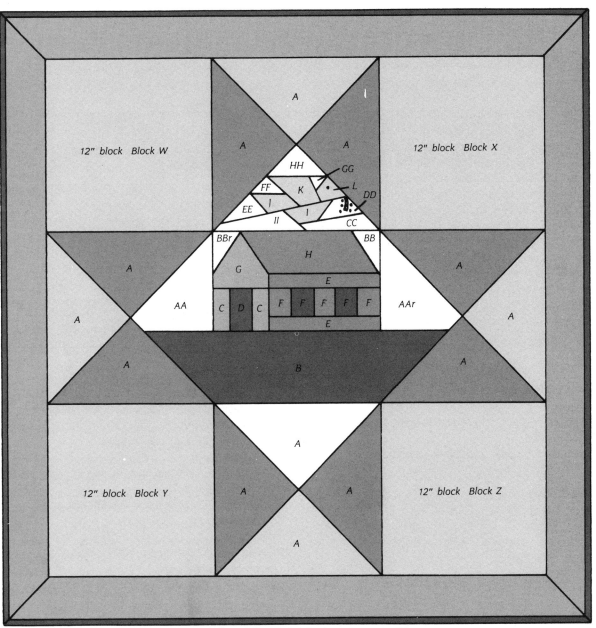

A variation of Noah's Ark is shown on page 67.

Dark brown stripe . . . . ½ yard
   Binding 1½″ × 5⅛ yards, one D, two F
Light brown print . . . . ⅛ yard
   Two E, three F
Light brown stripe . . . . ⅛ yard
   One H
White solid . . . . ⅛ yard
   One each I, J, K, L
Rust solid . . . . ¼ yard
   Two C, one G
Off-white print . . . . 1 yard
   Four A, background patches for four 12″ animal blocks
   of your choice
Various fabrics . . . . scraps
   Patches for four 12″ animal blocks
Lining fabric . . . . 2⅝ yards
Batting . . . . 46″ × 46″
Notions: olive green embroidery floss

Assembly Instructions

Enlarge patterns (or draft your own) for four 12″ animal blocks of your choice. Using off-white print in background patches, complete four animal blocks. (Blocks are called W, X, Y, and Z in quilt drawing.)

Make center ark-and-dove block using patches as indicated in quilt drawing. Appliqué olive branch; satin stitch olives with olive green embroidery floss. Sew a light blue solid A to bottom of block. Sew gold/brown-stripe A's to the bottom and right-hand edges of Block W, to the bottom and left-hand edges of Block X, to the top and right-hand edges of Block Y, and to the top and left-hand edges of Block Z. Join the five blocks and remaining A triangles to complete the quilt center.

Add borders, mitering corners and trimming excess.

Assemble and baste quilt lining, batting, and quilt top. Quilt background in parallel lines approximately 1″ apart. Quilt "in the ditch" around all animal patches and next to border.

Finish the quilt with dark-brown-stripe binding.

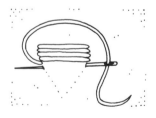

Satin Stitch

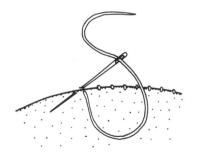

Blindstitch

Panda-Panda

Quilt Size: 31¾″ × 31¾″ for a wall hanging or baby quilt.

Yardage (44″ fabric) and Cutting Requirements

White solid . . . . ⅜ yard
   One each B, C, E, F, G, H, L, P, Q, R, T, U, V
Black solid . . . . ⅛ yard
   One each A, D, K, left eye, right eye, and nose
Black pindot . . . . ¼ yard
   One each I, J, M, N, O, S
Gray floral print . . . . ⅜ yard
   One each AA, BB, CC, DD, EE, FF, GG, HH, II, JJ, KK, LL, MM
Medium green solid . . . . ⅛ yard
   Eight X, eight Y
Dark green solid . . . . ¾ yard
   Four borders 1⅜″ × 32¼″, four borders 1⅜″ × 21¼″, binding 1½″ × 4 yards, forty-eight W
Dark green print . . . . ⅛ yard
   Forty-eight W
Light green print . . . . ¾ yard
   Sixteen NN, four OO, twelve PP, twelve PPr, four QQ, four QQr, four RR, four RRr, four SS, four SSr, eight TT, eight TTr, sixteen UU, four VV, four WW, eight WWr
Lining fabric . . . . 1⅛ yards
Batting . . . . 36″ × 36″

Assembly Instructions

Join block patches by hand as indicated in quilt drawing. (Patches C and S will require a clip halfway into the seam allowances at the indentations.) Ear patches A and D should be prepared for appliqué by turning under and basting the curved edges. Insert basted ears in seams, joining B-C and C-E as indicated on patterns. Using a blindstitch, appliqué curved edges of ears as well as eyes and nose. (Placement lines for eyes and nose are indicated on patterns with dotted lines.)

Sew a short dark-green solid border to each edge of panda block, mitering corners and trimming excess to leave ¼″ seam allowances.

Patch letters for one border are given in quilt drawing. (All four borders are identical.) Lay out patches for one border as shown, checking carefully that you have patches in correct position. (PP, QQ, SS, and WW are easily confused because they are similar.)

Make "bamboo" units from UU-X-UU and TT-Y-TTr patches. Sew dark green solid W's alternately with dark green print W's to make "bamboo leaves" units. Join units and other patches to complete border. Repeat to make four borders in the same way.

Sew borders to quilt top, beginning at the ends with the VV patches and leaving the last few inches unsewn. After joining all four borders to panda block, sew the last few inches of the seams joining pieced borders and strip borders, and join the corner "bamboo leaves" units to adjacent border. Add remaining dark green borders, mitering corners.

Panda-Panda is shown on the Front Cover.

Lightly press the quilt top as follows: press seam allowances around edges of panda toward center of animal (seam allowances on B, E, F, G, and H should be pressed toward center of head), press seam allowances on leg patches J, M, and S toward center of each leg, press seam allowances of dark-green strip borders toward center of borders, and press seam allowances on X and Y patches toward background fabric.

Assemble and baste quilt lining, batting, and quilt top. Quilt "in the ditch" around all patches of panda block, next to strip borders, and on long edges of X and Y patches. Quilt through the center of each dark-green print W. Outline quilt ¼" from seams around bamboo leaves.

Add ¼" seam allowances to all patches, except add ³⁄₁₆" turn-under allowance to eyes and nose. Dimensions given for border strips include seam allowances.

Finish the quilt with dark-green solid binding.

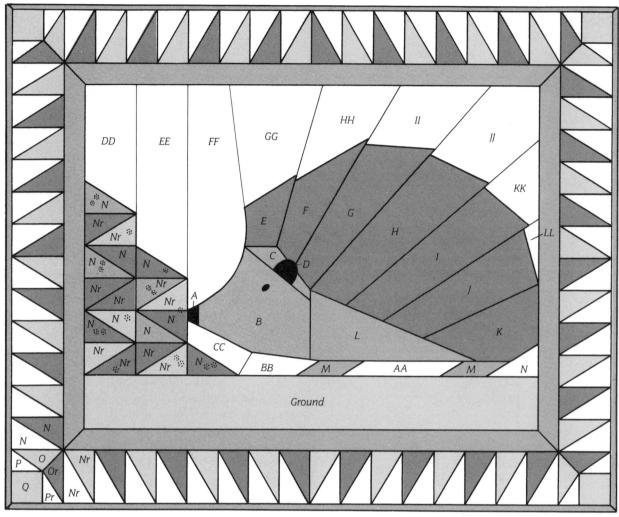

Raspberries for Supper is shown on page 72.

Raspberries for Supper

Quilt Size: 29" × 23" for a wall hanging.

Yardage (44" fabric) and Cutting Requirements

Dark brown print . . . . ¼ yard
  One each E, F, G, H, I, J, K
Brown solid . . . . scrap
  One A, two D
Medium brown print . . . . ¼ yard
  One B, one C, one L, two M
Light brown print . . . . ⅛ yard
  One piece 3" × 22½" for ground
Dark pink stripe . . . . ⅛ yard
  Fourteen N, fourteen Nr, four Or
Medium pink print . . . . ⅜ yard
  Binding 1½" × 3⅜ yards, 2 borders 1½" × 24½", 2 borders 1½" × 18½"
Light pink print . . . . ⅛ yard
  Fourteen N, fourteen Nr, four O, four Q
Green prints . . . . scraps
  Nine N, ten Nr

White/pink print . . . . ½ yard
  One each AA, BB, CC, DD, EE, FF, GG, HH, II, JJ, KK, LL, twenty-nine N, twenty-eight Nr, four P, four Pr
Lining fabric . . . . ⅞ yard
Batting . . . . 33" × 27"
Notions: brown and white embroidery floss; pink #3 perle cotton

Assembly Instructions

Join block patches in units as follows: five green print N's, six green print Nr's, and white/pink DD for left side of quilt block; three green print N's, four green print Nr's, and white/pink EE. Join green print N and CC, BB, M, AA, and M for area below hedgehog body. Join E-GG; F-HH; G-II; H-JJ; I-KK; and J-LL.

Sew curved edges of the D patches with wrong sides together; turn right sides out. Insert D in seam joining B and C, folding in edges ⅛". Add nose patch A. Join units and patches FF, K, L, and a white/pink N. Add the ground piece.

Add medium pink print borders, mitering corners and trimming excess.

Join N and Nr patches as shown in quilt drawing for borders. Sew a short border to each side of quilt top, placing borders so the pink patches point away from hedgehog block. Join O, Or, P, Pr, and Q patches for corner units of borders; sew one corner unit to each end of long borders. Sew long borders to top and bottom edges of quilt top, placing borders so the pink patches point away from hedgehog block.

Embroider eye with brown floss in satin stitch; embroider outline of eye with white embroidery floss in outline stitch. Using #3 perle cotton, embroider raspberries on bush as shown in quilt drawing. (Each raspberry is made with seven French knots.)

Lightly press seam allowances around edges of hedgehog away from background, press edges of green "bush" patches away from background, and press pink border-strip pieces toward center of strip borders.

Assemble and baste quilt lining, batting, and quilt top. Outline quilt ¼" from seams on patches as desired, and quilt "in the ditch" on both sides of pink strip borders.

Finish the quilt with medium pink print binding.

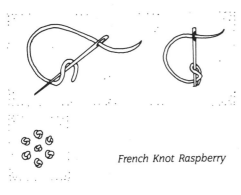

French Knot Raspberry

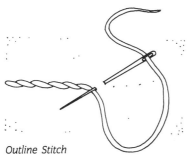

Outline Stitch

Satin Stitch

Scottie Quilt

Quilt Size: 81¼" × 98⅛" for a double bed quilt.
Block Size: 10".

Yardage (44" fabric*) and Cutting Requirements

Red plaid . . . . .3 yards
    Two borders 5½" × 98⅝", two borders 5½" × 81¼", eighty sashes 2½" × 10½"
Black solid . . . . .2¼ yards
    Binding 1½" × 10¾ yards, thirty-two F, thirty-two G, thirty-two H, forty-nine setting squares cut 2½" × 2½"
Green solid . . . . .⅝ yard
    Thirty-two D
Blue/green plaid . . . . .1 yard
    Thirty-two E
Gray solid . . . . .3¾ yards
    Fourteen A, four B, thirty-two C, thirty-two I, thirty-two J, thirty-two K, thirty-two L
Red solid . . . . .¼ yard
    Thirty-two 1" × 6" bias strips for collars
Lining fabric . . . . .5⅞ yards
Batting . . . . .85" × 102"
*Yardage for 60"-wide wool fabric is as follows: 3 yards red plaid; 1¾ yards black solid; ½ yard green solid; ⅝ yard blue/green plaid; 2⅜ yards gray solid; ¼ yard red solid; lining, 5½ yards (seamed horizontally); 85" × 102" batting.

Assembly Instructions

Join patches E and L; add H and G.

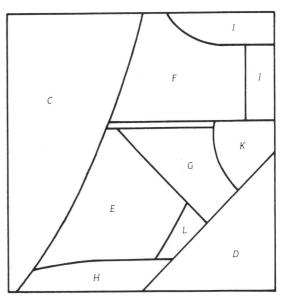

Scottie Block Drawing

Fold 1" red solid collar strip in half lengthwise; press. Pin collar strip to long edge of G, aligning raw edges, and baste as shown in Fig. 1. Sew K to curved edge of G.

Join patches F and J; add I. Sew this unit to body of dog. Add D and C to complete block. Repeat to make thirty-two blocks.

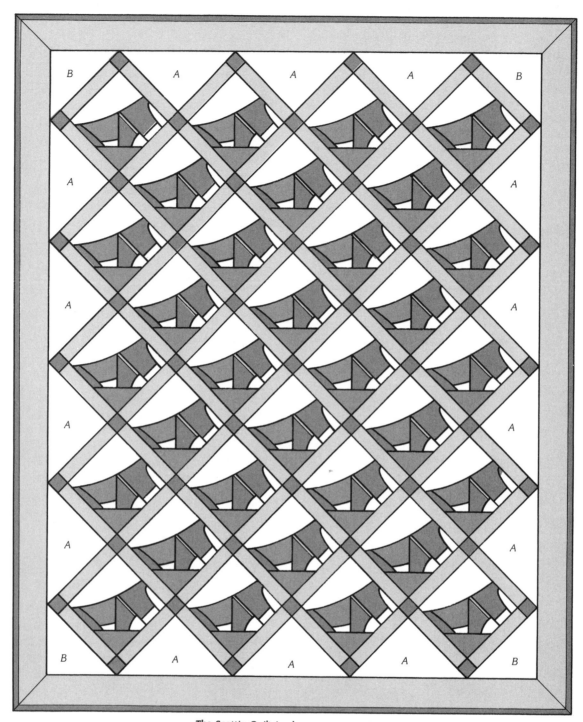

The Scottie Quilt is shown on page 68.

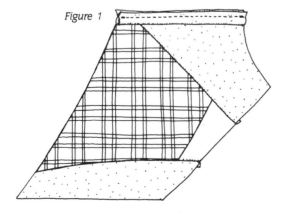

Figure 1

Join sashes, setting squares, blocks, A's, and B's as shown in quilt drawing, working in diagonal rows. Press sash seams away from blocks.

Add borders, mitering corners and trimming excess to leave ¼" seam allowances.

Assemble and baste quilt lining, batting, and quilt top. Quilt "in the ditch" around all patches. Quilt straight lines parallel to borders in A and B patches, and quilt border along lines of plaid.

Finish the quilt with black solid binding.

If desired, buttons may be added for Scotties' eyes.

Sit Up and Beg

Pillow Size: 14½″ plus 3″ ruffle
Block Size: 10″.

Yardage (44″ fabric) and Cutting Requirements

Light blue solid . . . . ¼ yard
   One each C, D, I, J, K, L
Black solid . . . . ¼ yard
   One each F, G, H, four corner squares cut 3″ × 3″
Blue/green plaid . . . . scrap
   One E
Red pindot . . . . ⅞ yard
   Two 15½″ squares for pillow back (double fabric for
   strength). Three ruffle strips 3″ × 44″, 1¼″ × 6″ bias strip
   for collar
Red/green plaid . . . . ⅝ yard
   Three ruffle strips 5″ × 44″, four borders 3″ × 10½″
Muslin . . . . 15″ × 15″
Batting . . . . 15½″ × 15½″
Notions: red embroidery floss, one black button, polyester
   stuffing or a 15″ pillow form

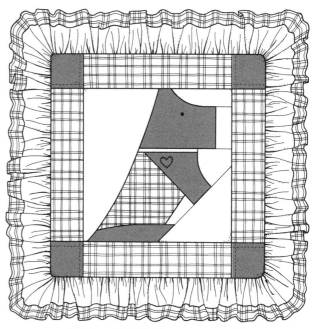

Sit Up and Beg is shown on page 69.

Assembly Instructions

Join patches E and L; add H and G.

Fold 1¼″ red pindot collar strip in half lengthwise with wrong sides together; press. Pin collar strip to long edge of G, aligning raw edges, and baste as shown in Fig. 1. Sew K to curved edge of G.

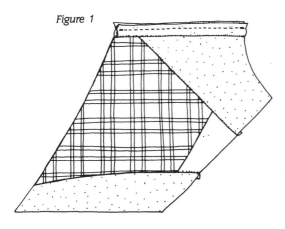

Figure 1

Join patches F and J; add I. Sew this unit to body of dog. Add D and C to complete block.

Sew a plaid border to two opposite edges of quilt block. Sew corner squares to each end of remaining borders; sew to quilt block.

Using red floss, backstitch a small heart on G.

Embroidered Heart for G Patch

Assemble and baste muslin, batting, and quilt block. Quilt as desired. Sew on button for eye.

Join ends of red pindot ruffle strips to make a long band. Join ends of plaid strips to make a long band. Join pindot band to plaid band. Seam the ends to make a continuous band as in Fig. 2. Fold band in half lengthwise, with right sides out, and press.

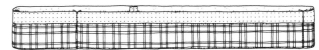

Figure 2

With pins, mark off ruffle into four equal segments. Sew two rows of machine basting (¼″ and ½″ from raw edge) between each pinned segment as in Fig. 3. Pull up thread to form gathers.

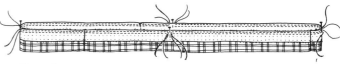

Figure 3

Pin gathered ruffle to right side of quilt block (with pindot band touching block), matching a pin to the center of each side. Baste ruffle in place.

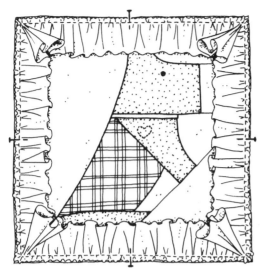

Figure 4

Pin *both* pillow back squares to right side of quilt block. Sew around ½" from edge, leaving a 4" opening. Turn pillow right sides out through opening. Stuff pillow, and close opening with small blindstitches.

Stormstown Cows

Quilt Size: 37½" × 37½" for a wall hanging or child's quilt.

Yardage (44" fabric) and Cutting Requirements

Black print . . . . ⅜ yard
   Sixteen A, sixteen B, forty-eight F
Black/white gingham check . . . . ¼ yard
   Sixteen A, sixteen C
Black solid . . . . ¼ yard
   Four strips 1¾" × 15½", forty-eight F
Black pindot . . . . ½ yard
   Binding 1½" × 4½ yards, forty-eight G
Gold print . . . . ½ yard
   Four A, thirty-two D, sixteen E, 116 G
Green/red print . . . . ⅝ yard
   Four strips 1¾" × 15½", sixteen F, 164 G
Green/yellow print . . . . ¾ yard
   Four strips 1¾" × 25½", sixteen F, twelve H, twenty-four J, sixteen K
White solid . . . . ⅜ yard
   Forty-eight F, twenty-four G, twenty-four I, twenty-four Ir
White/blue print . . . . ¼ yard
   Four strips 1¾" × 23"
Lining fabric . . . . 1¼ yards
Batting 41½" × 41½"
Notions: black and white embroidery floss

Assembly Instructions

Refer to photo in the Color Section to check fabric placement. As shown in block drawing for Farmer's Fields, make four blocks. Join the four blocks for quilt center.

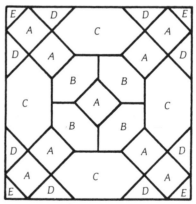

Farmer's Fields block

Make four nine-patch blocks using five black print F's and four green/red print F's in each; set aside. Make four sawtooth borders with twelve black pindot G's and twelve green/red print G's in each. Sew a black solid strip to the black pindot side of each sawtooth border; sew a green/red print strip to the green/red print side of each border. Sew one of these borders to each of two opposite sides of the quilt center, placing black strip of border next to Farmer's Fields blocks. Sew a black print/green print nine-patch block to each end of the two remaining borders; sew to quilt top.

The Stormstown Cows quilt is shown on page 40.

Sew white/blue print strips to two opposite edges of quilt top. Sew a black print F to each end of remaining white/blue strips; join to quilt top.

Sew green/yellow print strips to two opposite edges of quilt top. Sew a black print F to each end of remaining green/yellow strips; join to quilt top.

Make four nine-patch blocks using five black print F's and four green/yellow print F's in each; set aside. As shown in block drawing, make twelve cow blocks. (Cows' legs are appliquéd on J patches using a blindstitch.) Join four green/yellow print K's alternately with three cow blocks; repeat to make four borders like this. Sew a cow border to each of two opposite sides of the quilt top. Sew a black print/green print nine-patch block to each end of remaining cow borders; join to quilt top.

Make outer sawtooth border using twenty-eight green/red print G's and twenty-eight gold print G's; repeat to make four borders like this. Placing green print edge next to cow borders, sew a sawtooth border to each of two opposite edges of quilt top. Join a green/red print G to a yellow G for corner square; repeat to make four corner squares. Sew a corner square to each end of remaining sawtooth borders; join borders to quilt top.

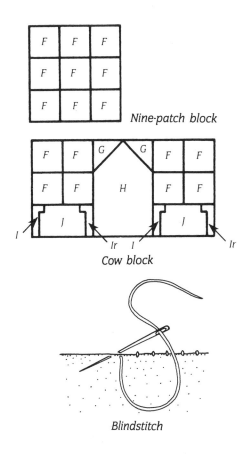

Nine-patch block

Cow block

Blindstitch

Embroider details on cows (as shown in quilt drawing) as follows: Use white floss to embroider tails in chain stitch and ends of tails in outline stitch; embroider horns in outline stitch. Use black floss to embroider eyes and nostrils with French knots and ears in outline stitch.

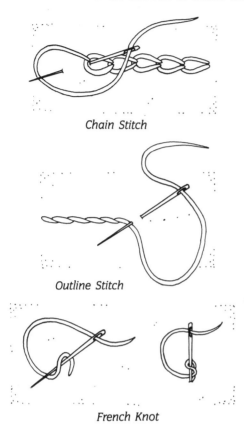

Chain Stitch

Outline Stitch

French Knot

Lightly press the quilt top.

Using a pencil or water-erasable marking pen, lightly mark a crescent moon in each H patch. In white/blue print strips, mark a "sun" in the center with four "clouds" on each side of the sun (as shown in quilt drawing).

Assemble and baste quilt lining, batting, and quilt top. Quilt Farmer's Fields blocks as desired. Quilt "in the ditch" around triangles in borders, around squares in nine-patch blocks, and around each cow. Quilt next to each cow tail. Quilt moon, sun, and cloud designs as marked.

Finish the quilt with black pindot binding.

Teddy Bear

Quilt Size: 18″ × 18″ for a wall hanging or doll quilt.

Yardage (44″ fabric) and Cutting Requirements

Dark brown stripe . . . . ⅜ yard
  Bias binding 1½″ × 2¼ yards
Dark brown print . . . . ⅛ yard
  One each C, Cr, H, Hr, J, Jr, K, Kr
Dark brown pindot . . . . ½ yard
  One each A, B, Br, D, E, Er, F, G, Gr, I, Ir, and twenty each
  of II, IIr, JJ, JJr
Red solid . . . . ⅛ yard
  Ten L, ten Lr, one small heart
Red print . . . . ⅛ yard
  Ten L, 10 Lr
White/red print . . . . ¼ yard
  One each AA, BB, BBr, CC, CCr, DD, DDr, EE, EEr, FF, FFr,
  GG, GGr, HH
Black solid . . . . scrap
  One nose, two eyes
Lining fabric . . . . ⅝ yard
Batting . . . . 22″ × 22″
Notions: black embroidery floss

Assembly Instructions

Join patches by hand to complete the teddy bear block. (Notches on curved patches should be marked in patch seam allowances. Sew from notch to notch to assure perfect alignment of seam lines.) Appliqué eyes, nose, and heart using a blind stitch. Using black floss, embroider mouth lines in outline stitch.

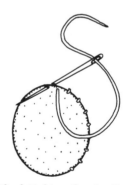

Blindstitching the Appliqués

For border, make ten heart blocks with red print on the right-hand side of heart; make ten heart blocks with red print on the left-hand side of heart. Join blocks to make border as shown in quilt drawing; sew borders to teddy bear block.

Assemble and baste quilt lining, batting, and quilt top. Outline quilt ¼″ outside teddy bear, inside each pieced heart, and inside seam joining block and border. Quilt "in the ditch" next to seams joining head, arms, and legs to body of teddy bear.

Finish the quilt with brown stripe bias binding.

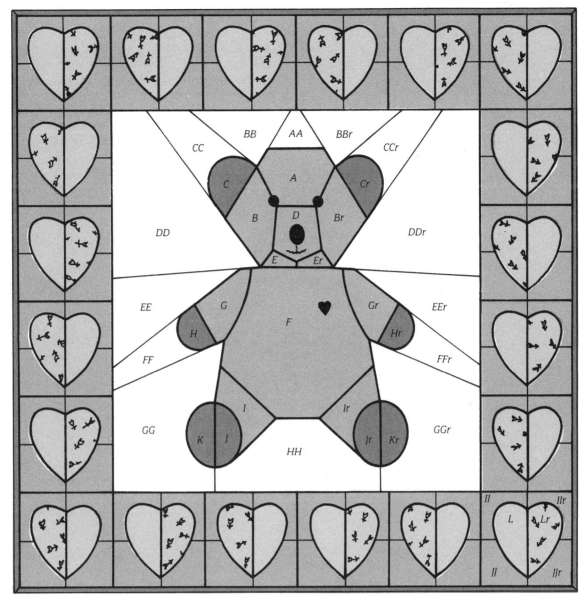

The Teddy Bear is shown on page 70.

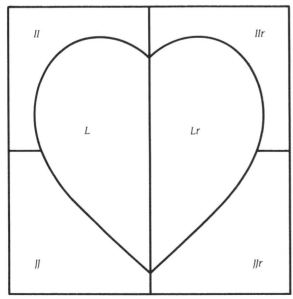

Border Heart

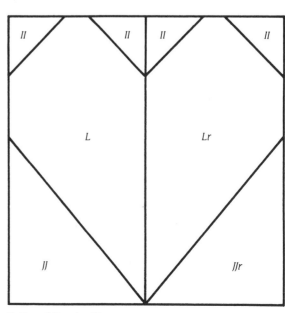

Optional Border Heart

85

The Chocolate Rabbit is shown on page 71.

The Chocolate Rabbit

Quilt Size: 17″ × 17″ for a wall hanging.

Yardage (44″ fabric) and Cutting Requirements

Medium brown print . . . . ¼ yard
One each of F, G, H, I, J, K, L, M, N, O, S, T, U, V, W, X, Y, a, b, c, d, and fifty-two border squares

Lighter medium brown print . . . . ⅛ yard
One each A, B, C, D, E, P, Q

Brown solid . . . . scrap
Mouth, nose, eyes

Dark peach solid . . . . ¼ yard
Binding 1½″ × 2¼ yards, four strips 1⅛″ × 13″

Light peach print . . . . ¼ yard
Eighty-four border squares

Light green solid . . . . ¼ yard
One each AA, BB, CC, DD, EE, FF, GG, HH, II, JJ, KK, LL, MM, NN, OO, PP, QQ, RR, SS, TT, UU, VV, WW

Light green print . . . . ⅛ yard
Thirty-two border squares

White print . . . . scrap
One each R, Z, e

Lining fabric . . . . 21″ × 21″

Batting . . . . 21″ × 21″

Notions: brown embroidery floss

86

Assembly Instructions

Join patches with hand sewing as indicated in quilt drawing to complete the rabbit block. Sew a dark peach solid strip to each edge of quilt block, mitering corners and trimming excess.

Assemble the border squares row by row, referring to the photograph in the Color Section for color placement. (Border patches can be sewn either by hand or machine.)

Appliqué eyes on the A patch using a blindstitch.

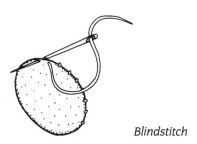

Blindstitch

Lightly press the quilt top, pressing seam allowances around the edges of the rabbit away from the background. Press seam allowances on dark peach border toward center of border (away from block and pieced border).

Using brown embroidery floss, embroider the outer edges of the rabbit's tail in outline stitch to make it show up against the light background fabric.

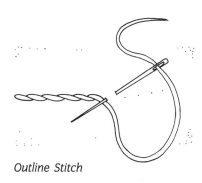

Outline Stitch

Assemble and baste quilt lining, batting, and quilt top. Quilt "in the ditch" around the edges of the rabbit, around the haunch patches (P and Q), around the head, and around Z and e patches. Quilt "in the ditch" between other block patches as desired. Quilt the pieced border in diagonal lines through the center of all patches.

Finish the quilt with dark peach binding.

The Zoo Quilt

Quilt Size: 42″ × 52″ for a crib quilt.

Yardage (44″ fabric) and Cutting Requirements

Dark green print . . . . ⅞ yard
  Fifty-two A, ninety-two C, fourteen E, fourteen Er, four G, four Gr, four I, four Ir, eight K

Medium green solid . . . . 1⅝ yards
  Two borders 1½″ × 52½″, two borders 1½″ × 42½″, two borders 1½″ × 40½″, two borders 1½″ × 30½″, binding 1½″ × 5¾ yards

Light blue print . . . . ¾ yard
  Sixty-four B, fifty-six C, fourteen D, fourteen Dr, fourteen F, fourteen Fr, four H, four Hr, four J, four Jr

Pale green solid . . . . .1 yard
  Background patches for quilt blocks

Yellow and gold prints and solids . . . . scraps
  Thirty-six strips 1″ × 44″ for sashes

Various prints and solids . . . . scraps
  Patches for quilt blocks

Lining fabric . . . . .3¼ yards

Batting . . . . .46″ × 56″

Assembly Instructions

Choose any animal blocks for your zoo. Enlarge patterns from those given, or draft your own. Dimensions for blocks (finished size, not including seam allowances) are given in the quilt drawing. Make blocks of your choice in these dimensions, or make blocks that will finish (when joined with sashes) to be 28″ × 38″.

To make sashes, join the thirty-six 1″ × 44″ yellow and gold strips to make "yardage" about 18″ × 44″ as shown in Fig. 1. Cut sashes in dimensions shown in quilt drawing (or in dimensions of your choice), remembering to add ¼″ seam allowances.

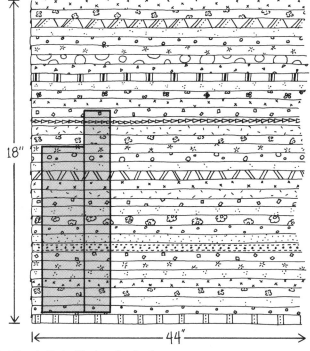

Fig. 1, Strip Piecing for Sashes

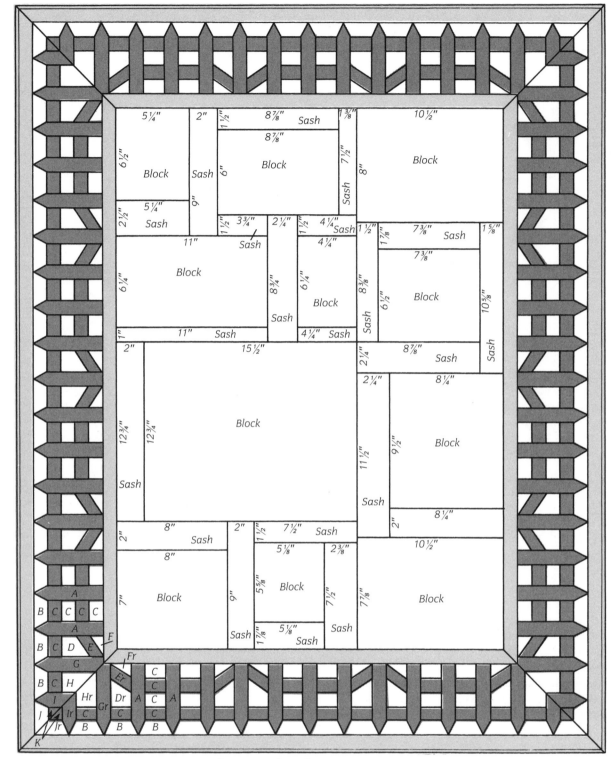

The Zoo Quilt is shown on page 38.

Join blocks and sashes to make the quilt top 28″ × 38″. Sew the 1½″ × 30½″ green borders to top and bottom of quilt top; sew the 1½″ × 40½″ borders to sides of quilt top. Miter corners, trimming excess to leave ¼″ seam allowances.

Join border "fence" patches as indicated by patch letters in quilt drawing. Press seam allowances away from fence background patches. Complete the four fence borders, then sew borders to quilt top. Sew the 1½″ × 42½″ border strips to top and bottom of quilt top; sew the 1½″ × 52½″ borders to sides. Miter corners, trimming excess to leave ¼″ seam allowances. Press seam allowances on green border strips toward middle of strips.

Embroider details and lettering as desired.

Assemble and baste quilt lining, batting, and quilt top. Quilt "in the ditch" next to each animal. Quilt block background patches along seam lines and as you wish. Quilt details in blocks as desired. Quilt "in the ditch" next to border strips and on both sides of all "fence" patches.

Finish the quilt with medium green binding.

Appendix
Enlarging Patterns

The ability and willingness to enlarge patterns to the optimum size will open up countless opportunities for quiltmakers. It is simply not possible to offer every pattern in every size. However, enlarging patterns is so easy that there is no reason why every quiltmaker, beginner or advanced, cannot learn to enlarge graphed patterns.

The fifty animal block drawings in this book have two sets of grid lines marked around the edges of the blocks. The inner set of marks divides the block into ten equal divisions; the outer set of markings divides the block into twelve equal divisions. These markings will help you enlarge the blocks to 10″ or 12″ by allowing 1″ for each division. By allowing 2″ for each grid square, the enlarged block would be either 20″ or 24″. By allowing 1½″ for each pattern square, the enlarged block would be 15″ or 18″. *The number of divisions multiplied by the enlarged size of each division equals the finished size of the enlarged block.*

To form a grid over the block drawing you want to enlarge, simply choose the number of divisions (ten or twelve), or divide the block into any number of divisions of your choice. Mark (in pencil!) to complete the grid over your block.

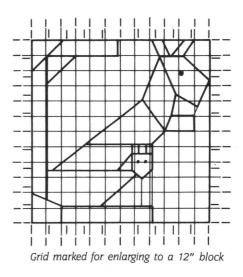

Grid marked for enlarging to a 12″ block

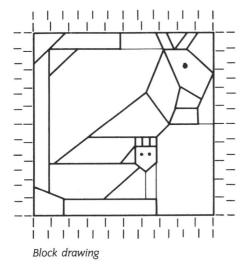

Block drawing

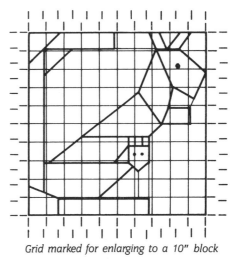

Grid marked for enlarging to a 10″ block

Now you will need a piece of graph paper large enough for your full-size block—probably a 10" or 12" square. The graph paper must have lines 1" apart (or whatever your "multiplying number" was when you decided how big to make your finished block). It's okay to use graph paper with more lines per inch, but the only lines you will use are the ones 1" apart. Most graph paper clearly shows the 1" lines—if not, mark over them lightly in pencil. Your big piece of graph paper should have exactly the same number of grid squares as your little block drawing.

When you begin enlarging your block design, don't concern yourself with the whole design. You only need to deal with one little grid square at a time. (Many of the grid squares of your block design will have nothing in them.) On the top row of grid squares on the block drawing, count over from the left to the square that has a design line through it. For the kangaroo block, the first square has part of the tail. Now find the same square on the big grid, and draw a line in the corresponding square to match the position and angle of the line in the little square.

Wasn't that easy? Even if your new line is in a slightly different place or at a slightly different angle, it will probably be close enough. Now mark the line(s) for the next grid square. Continue until all the squares with markings in the top row have been marked on the enlarged grid.

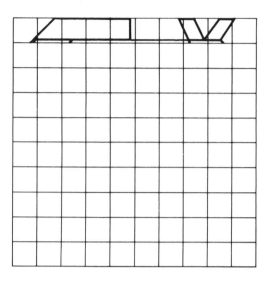

The remaining rows of the block are all marked the same way, until the design has been completed square by square.

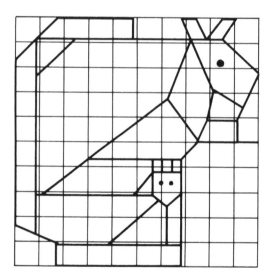

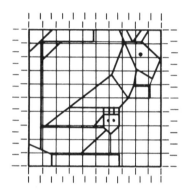

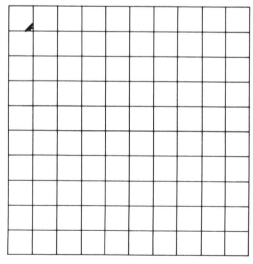

It's a good idea to hold your small and large designs at arm's length to check the overall accuracy of your enlarged design. It's also helpful to rotate both designs (the same way, of course) to look at the block with a different perspective. Make any corrections you decide would improve the enlarged pattern. Because it is sometimes difficult to tell which design lines are for animal patches and which are for background patches, it is helpful to lightly shade the patches as shown in the block drawing.

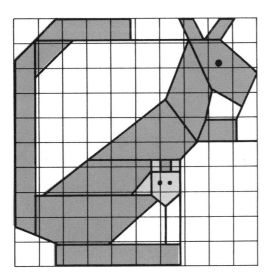

References for Further Reading

For General Design and Construction Tips

Beyer, Jinny. *Patchwork Patterns*. McLean, Va.: EPM Publications, 1979.

Beyer, Jinny. *The Quilter's Album of Blocks and Borders*. McLean, Va.: EPM Publications, 1980.

Hassel, Carla J. *You Can Be a Super Quilter!* Des Moines, Iowa: Wallace-Homestead, 1980.

Hassel, Carla J. *Super Quilter II*. Des Moines, Iowa: Wallace-Homestead, 1982.

James, Michael. *The Quiltmaker's Handbook*. Englewood Cliffs, N.J.: Prentice-Hall, Inc., 1978.

James, Michael. *The Second Quiltmaker's Handbook*. Englewood Cliffs, N.J.: Prentice-Hall, Inc. 1981.

Leman, Bonnie. *How to Make a Quilt: 25 Easy Lessons for Beginners*. Wheatridge, Colo.: Leman Publications, Inc., 1971.

Leman, Bonnie, Marie Shirer, and Susie Ennis. *Patchwork Sampler Legacy Quilt: Intermediate and Advanced Lessons in Patchwork*. 2nd rev. ed. Wheatridge, Colo.: Leman Publications, Inc., 1984.

Leone, Diana. *The Sampler Quilt, Book II*. Oak View, Calif.: Leone Publications, 1980.

Martin, Judy. *Patchworkbook: Easy Lessons for Quilt Design and Construction*. New York: Scribner's, 1983.

For Animal Design Ideas

Anderson, Sydney, ed. *Simon and Schuster's Guide to Mammals*. New York: Simon and Schuster, 1982.

Hamm, Jack. *How to Draw Animals*. New York: Putnam Publishing Group, 1969.

Holl, Adelaide. *All Kinds of Animals*. Racine, Wis.: Western Publishing Company, Inc., 1977.

Provensen, Alice and Martin. *A Peaceable Kingdom: The Shaker Abecedarius*. New York: Penguin Books, 1978.

To See Pieced Animal Designs

Aunt Kate's Quilting Bee. (Magazine is no longer being published. Mail order pattern service available from P.O. Box 113, Walnut Creek, Ohio 44687.

Bishop, Robert, William Secord, and Judith Reitner Weissman. *Quilts, Coverlets, Rugs and Samplers*. New York: Alfred A. Knopf, 1982.

Brackman, Barbara. *An Encyclopedia of Pieced Quilt Patterns, Volumes 1 and 2*. Lawrence, Kans.: Prairie Flower Publications, 1979-1984.

Burbidge, Pauline. *Making Patchwork for Pleasure and Profit*. London: John Gifford, Ltd., 1981.

Danner, Scioto Imhoff and Helen Ericson. *Mrs. Danner's Quilts* (mail-order catalog). Box 650, Emporia, Kans.

Dubois, Jean. *Bye Baby Bunting*. Evans, Colo.: La Plata Press, 1979.

Eitel, Jean, ed. *Quilt*. Harris Publications, Inc., New York. Published four times annually.

Houck, Carter, ed. *Lady's Circle Patchwork Quilts*. New York: Lopez Publications. Published six times annually.

Leman, Bonnie, ed. *Quilter's Newsletter Magazine*. Wheatridge, Colo.: Leman Publications, Inc. Published ten times annually.

Leman, Bonnie, ed. *Quiltmaker*. Wheatridge, Colo.: Leman Publications, Inc. Published twice annually.

Lockport Cotton Batting Co. *Lockport Quilting Pattern Book*. Lockport, N.Y.: Lockport Cotton Batting Co.

McKim, Ruby Short. *101 Patchwork Patterns*. New York: Dover Publications, 1962.

Parker, Kay. *Contemporary Quilts*. Trumansburg, N.Y.: The Crossing Press, 1981.

Simpson, Grace. *Quilts Beautiful: Their Stories and How to Make Them*. Winston-Salem, N.C.: Hunter Publishing Co., 1981. (Book available from Thimbles 'n Roses, P. O. Box 18524, Greensboro, North Carolina 27419.)

Swasey, Ruth, ed. *Stitch 'n Sew Quilts*. Seabrook, N.H.: House of White Birches. Published six times annually.

Vibert, Joan and Joyce Whittier. *At Grandma's Knee: A Collection of Doll Quilts*. Leawood, Kans.: Evening Star Farm, 1985.

Wilson, Erica. *Erica Wilson's Quilts of America*. Birmingham, Ala.: Oxmoor House, 1979.

Woodard, Thomas K. and Blanche Greenstein. *Crib Quilts and Other Small Wonders*. New York: E.P. Dutton, 1981.

Index to Creatures

Bold numbers indicate page numbers for graphed or full-size patterns in this book; other page numbers refer to a drawing or photograph. Other sources for animals are also given. See the References for Further Reading for complete information.

General Index

Bold entries indicate projects for which directions are given in this book.

Templates

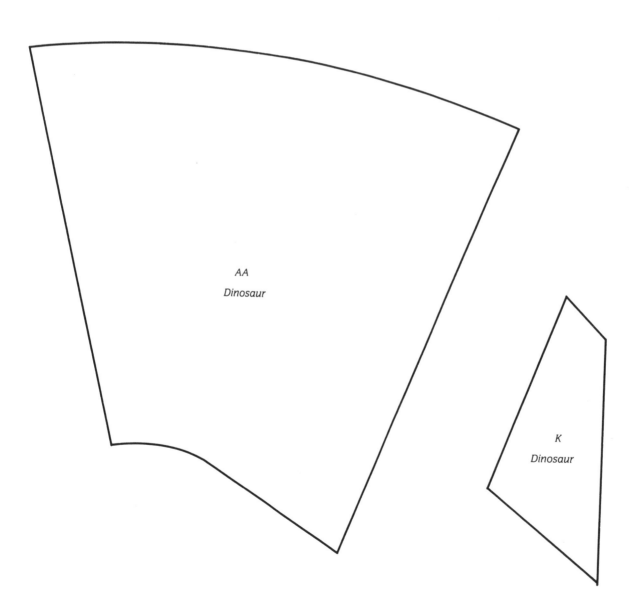

AA
Dinosaur

K
Dinosaur

Add ¼" seam allowances to all patches.

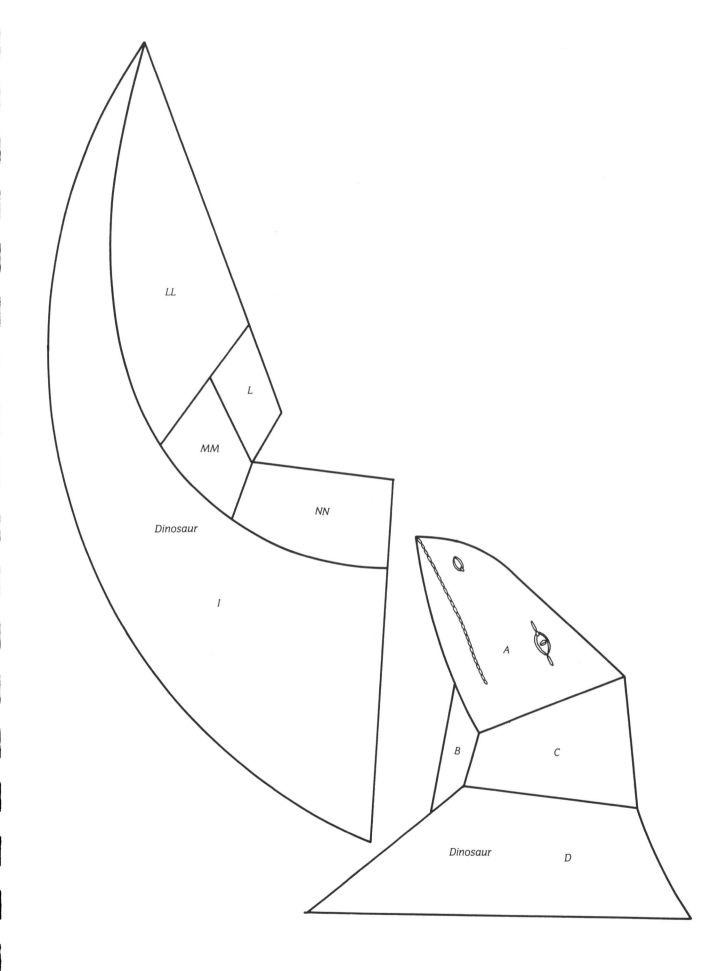

LL

L

MM

NN

Dinosaur

I

A

B

C

Dinosaur

D

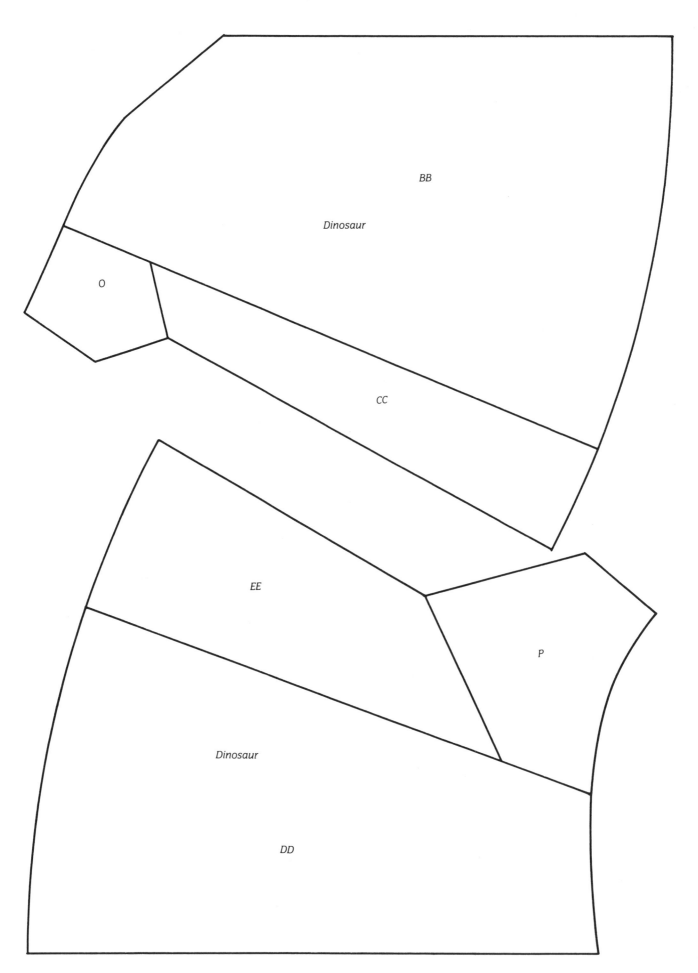

BB

Dinosaur

O

CC

EE

P

Dinosaur

DD

98

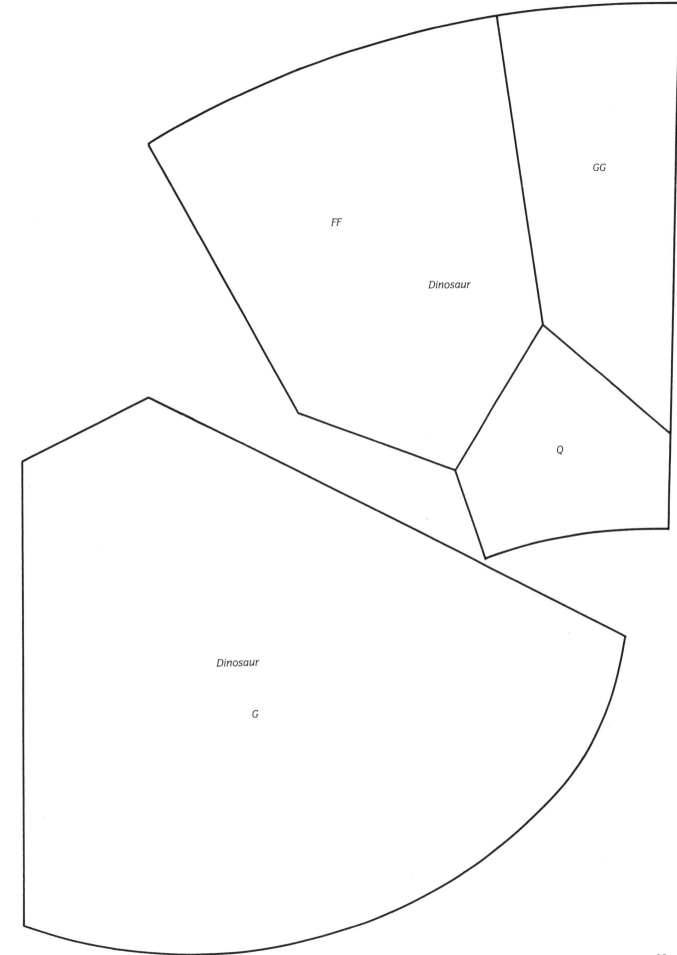

FF

GG

Dinosaur

Q

Dinosaur

G

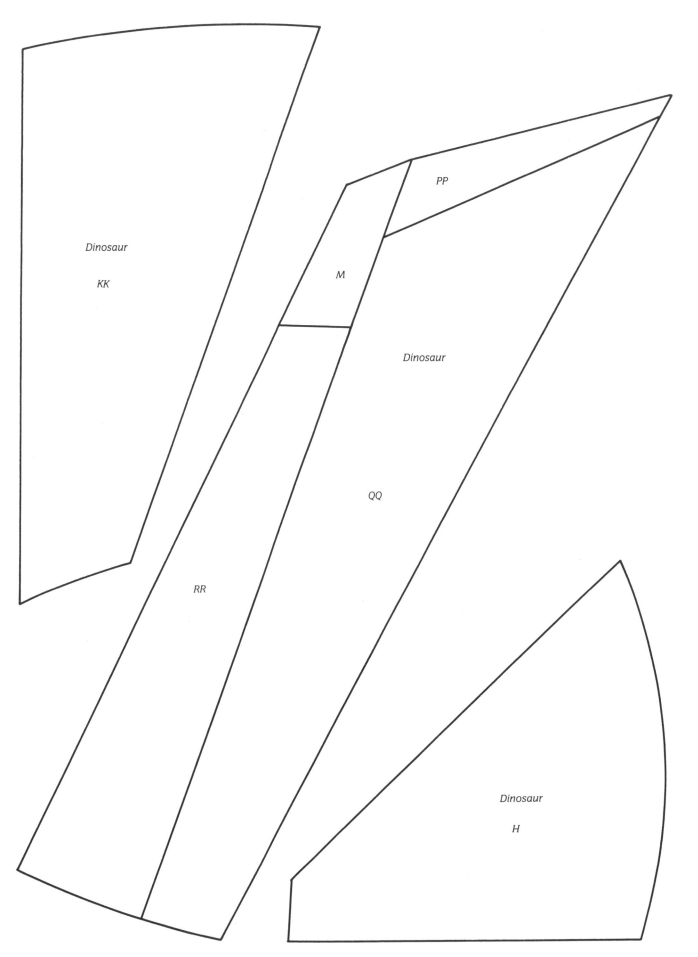

Dinosaur

KK

PP

M

Dinosaur

QQ

RR

Dinosaur

H

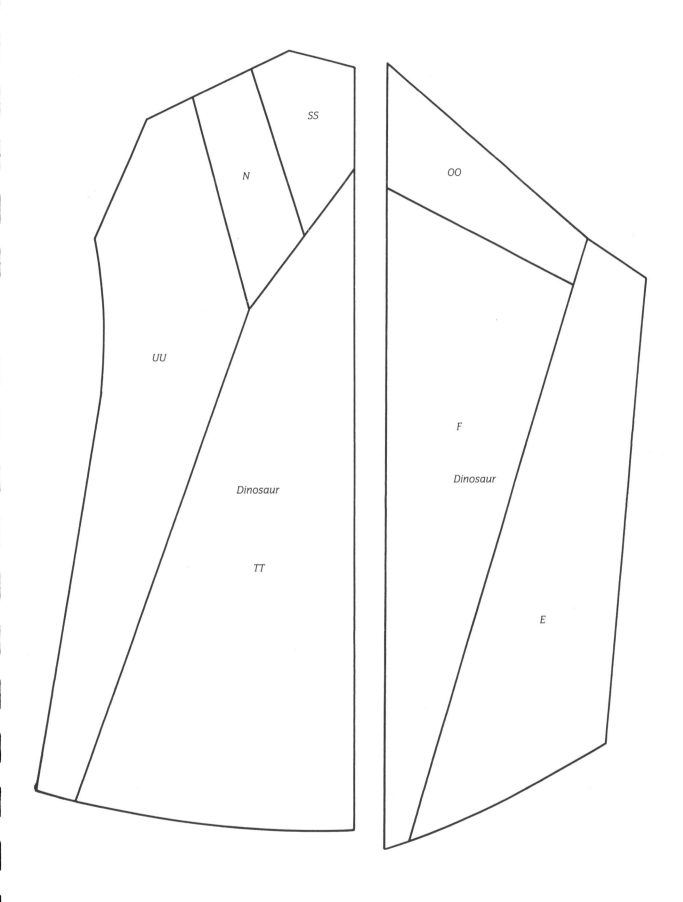

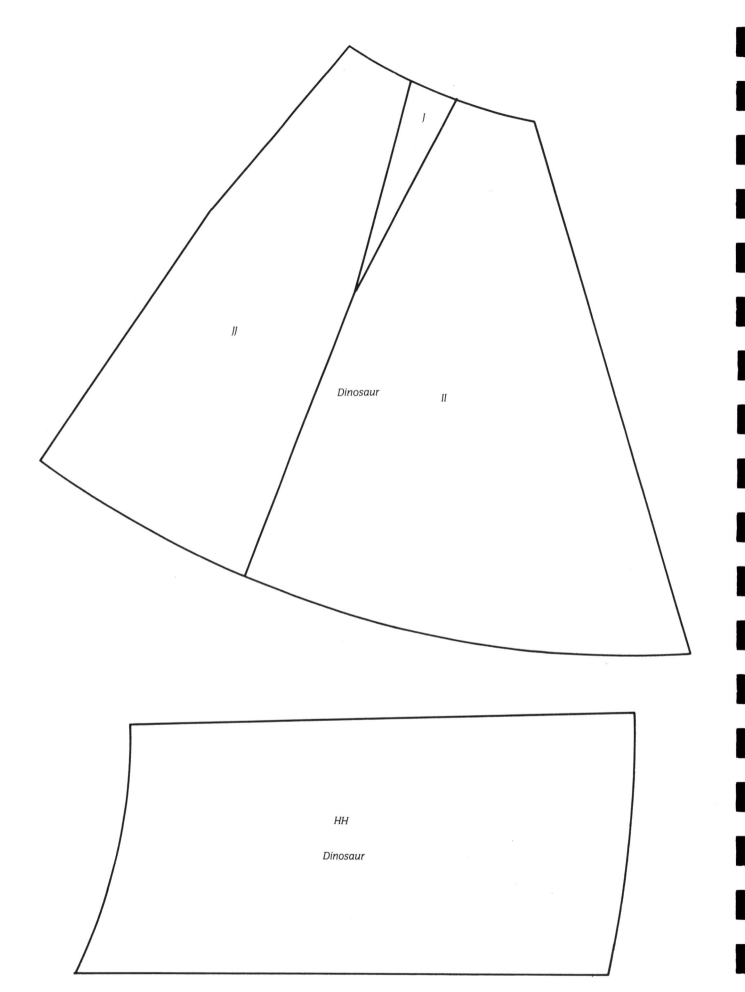

JJ

J

Dinosaur II

HH

Dinosaur

102

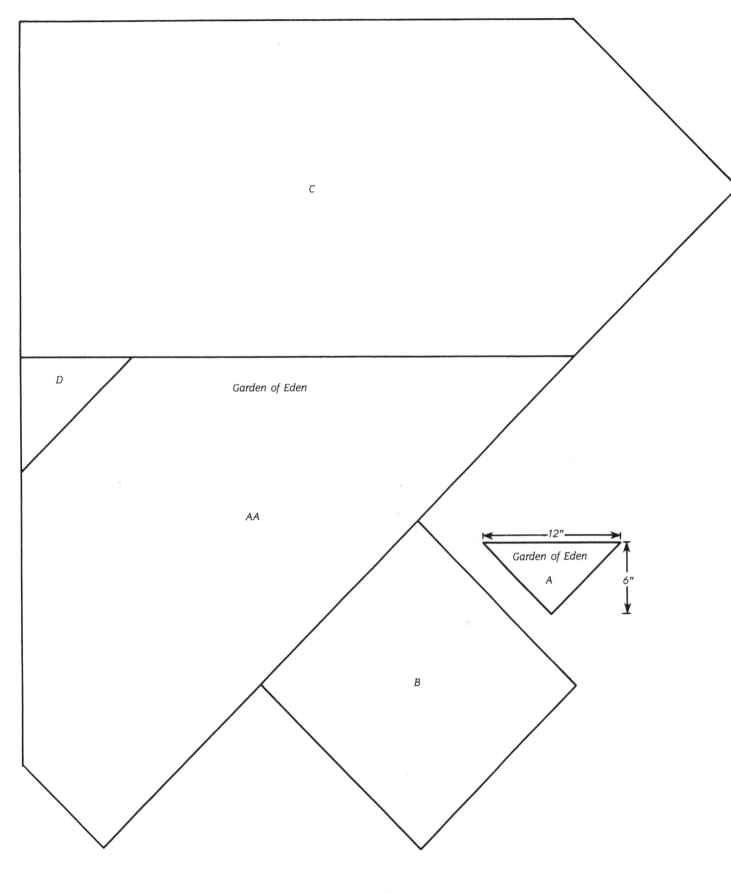

C

D

Garden of Eden

AA

Garden of Eden

A

B

12"

6"

Make full-size pattern for A by ruling a right triangle on graph paper in dimensions shown.

Add ¼" seam allowances to patches A, B, C, D, and AA.

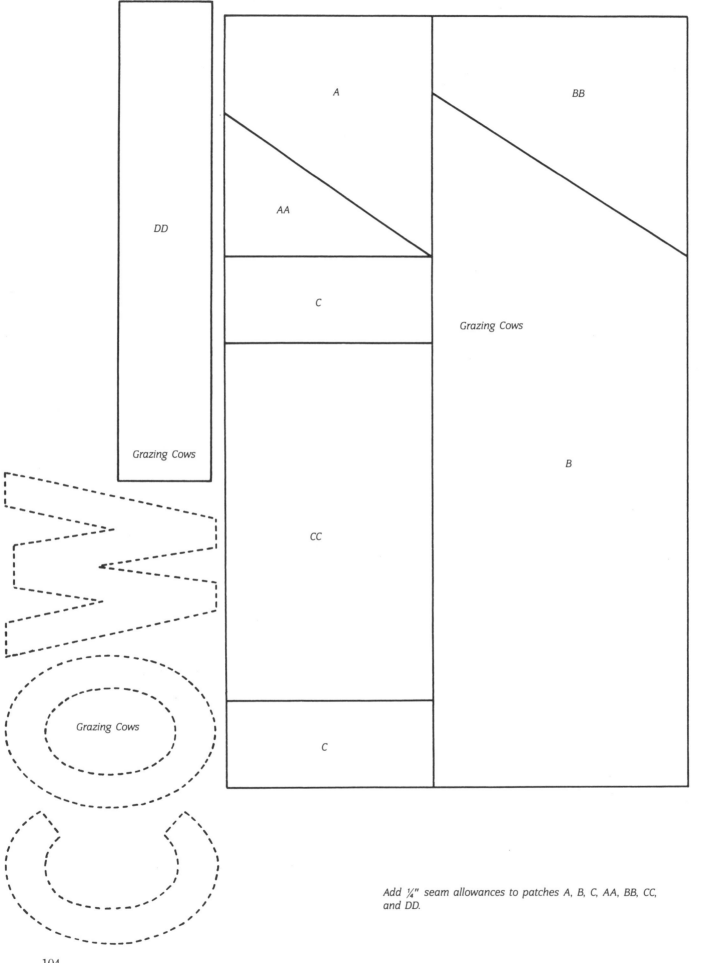

DD

A

BB

AA

C

Grazing Cows

Grazing Cows

CC

B

C

Grazing Cows

Add ¼" seam allowances to patches A, B, C, AA, BB, CC, and DD.

104

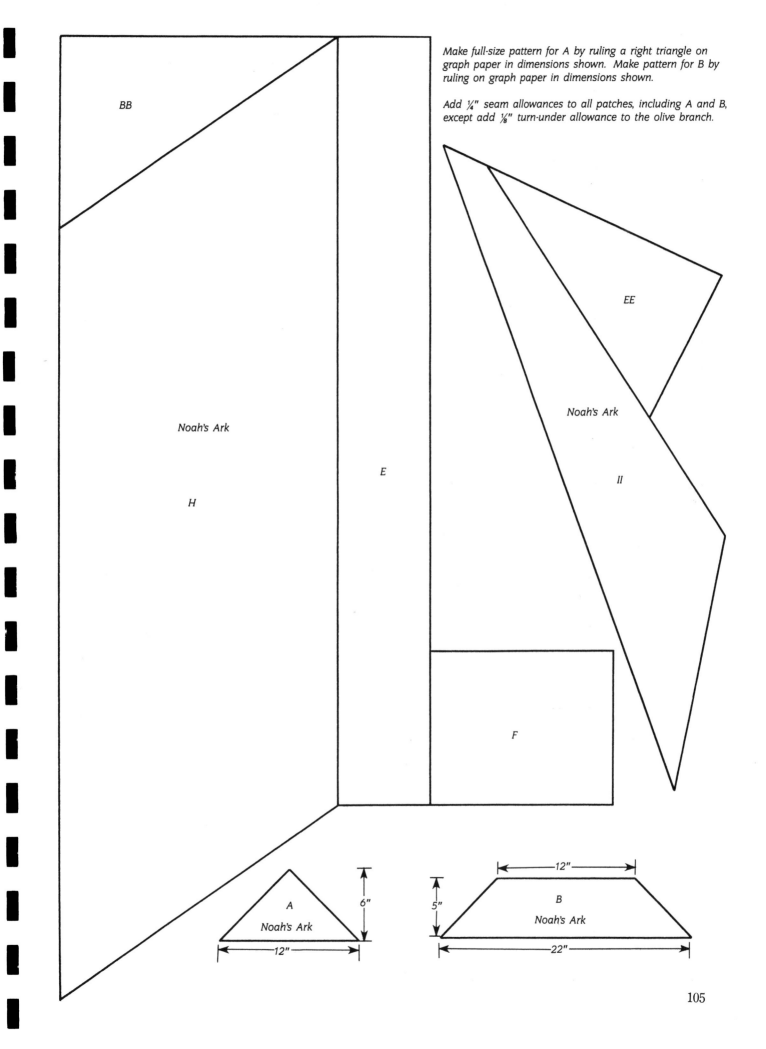

BB

Make full-size pattern for A by ruling a right triangle on graph paper in dimensions shown. Make pattern for B by ruling on graph paper in dimensions shown.

Add ¼″ seam allowances to all patches, including A and B, except add ⅛″ turn-under allowance to the olive branch.

Noah's Ark

H

E

EE

Noah's Ark

II

F

A

Noah's Ark

6″

12″

12″

B

Noah's Ark

5″

22″

105

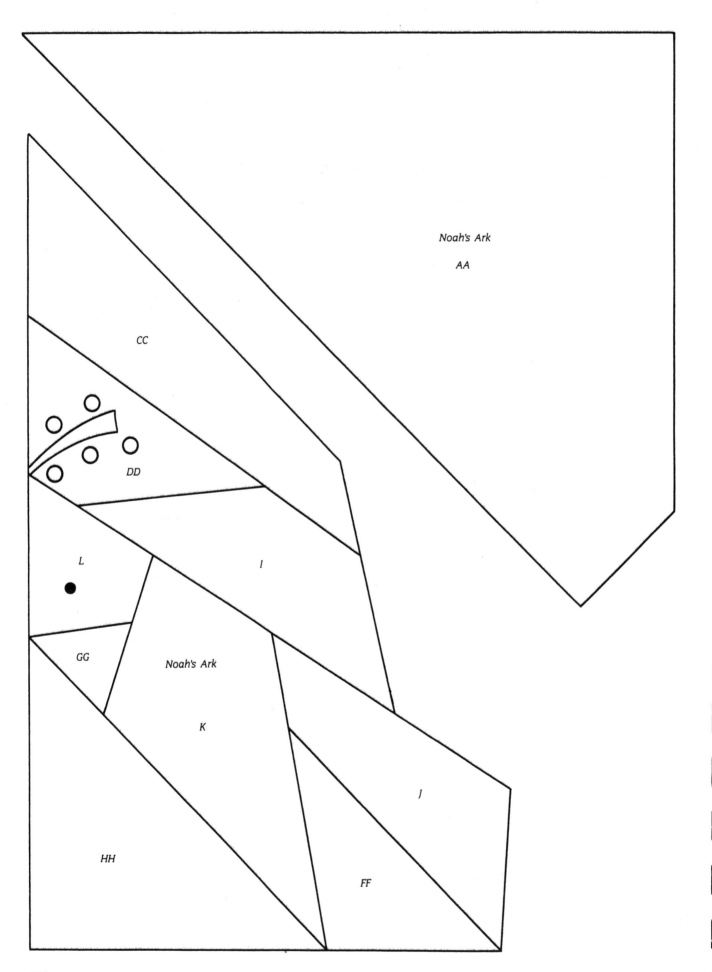

Noah's Ark

AA

CC

DD

L

I

GG

Noah's Ark

K

J

HH

FF

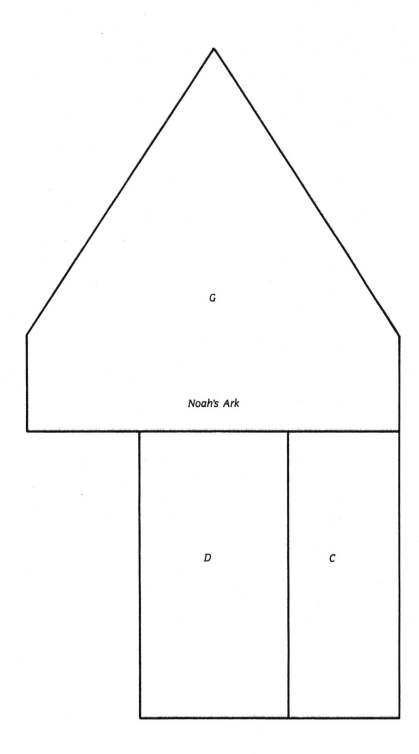

G

Noah's Ark

D   C

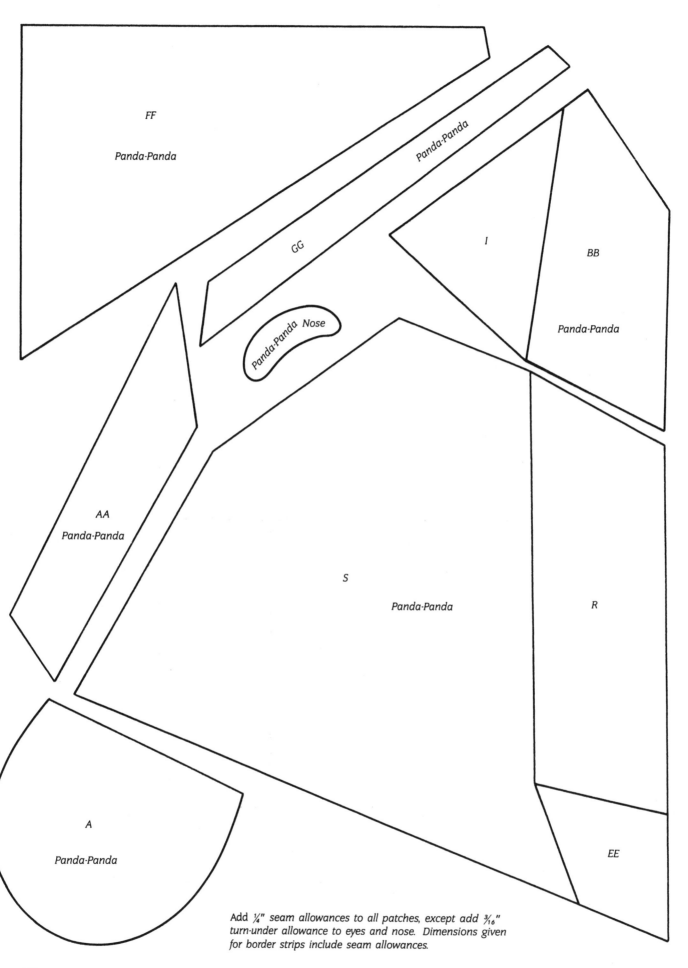

FF

Panda-Panda

Panda-Panda

GG

I

BB

Panda-Panda

Panda-Panda Nose

AA

Panda-Panda

S

Panda-Panda

R

A

Panda-Panda

EE

Add ¼" seam allowances to all patches, except add ³⁄₁₆"
turn-under allowance to eyes and nose. Dimensions given
for border strips include seam allowances.

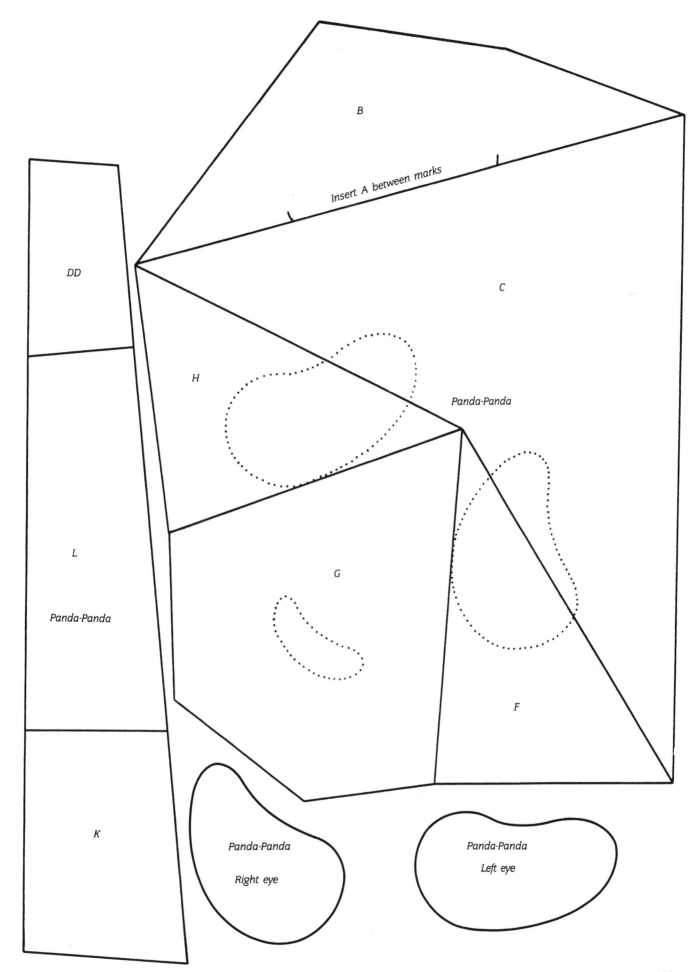

B

Insert A between marks

DD

C

H

Panda-Panda

L

Panda-Panda

G

Panda-Panda

F

K

Panda-Panda

Right eye

Panda-Panda

Left eye

109

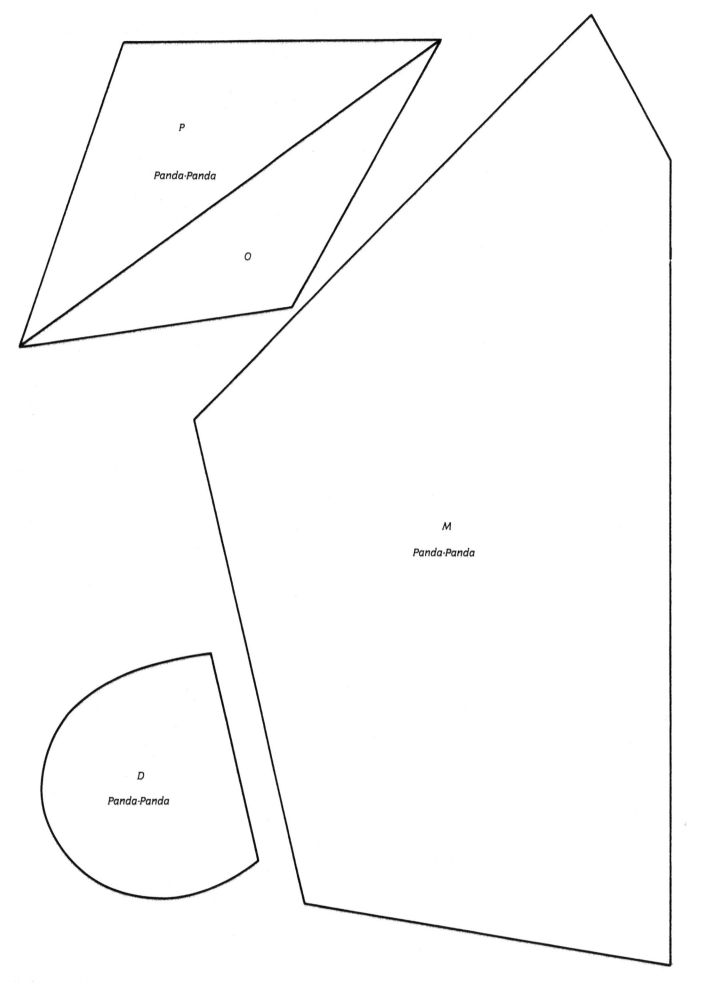

P

Panda-Panda

O

M

Panda-Panda

D

Panda-Panda

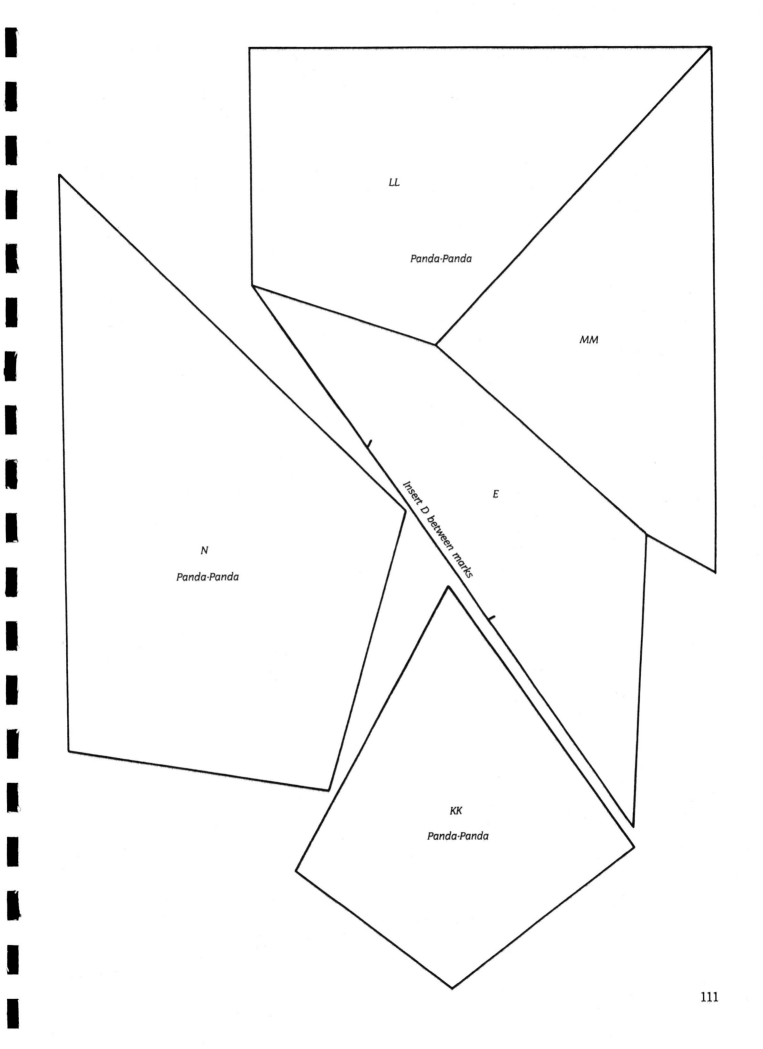

LL

Panda-Panda

MM

Insert D between marks

E

N

Panda-Panda

KK

Panda-Panda

111

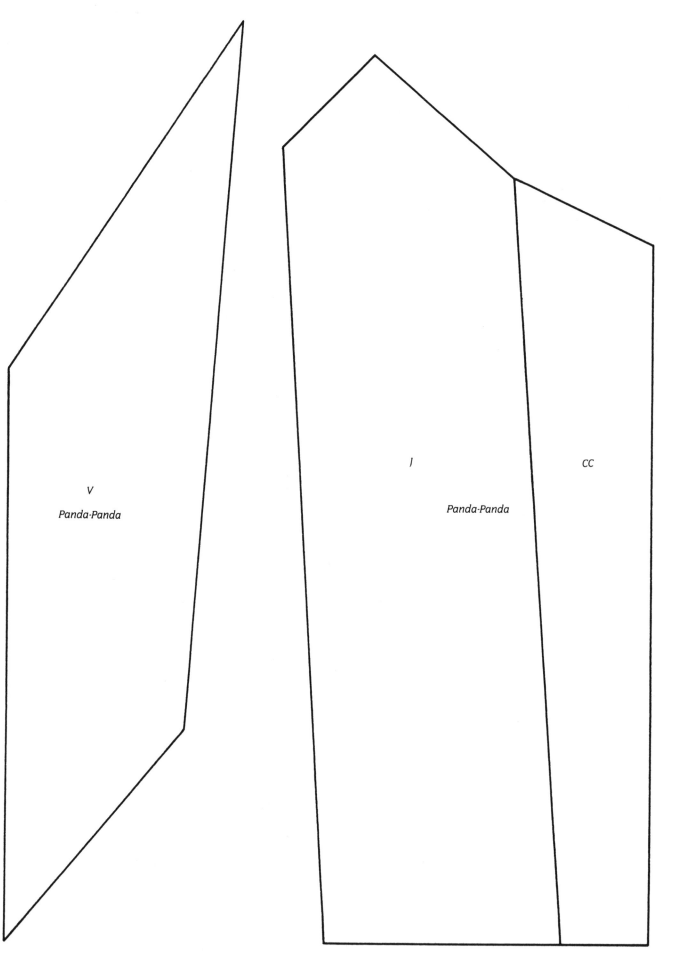

V

Panda-Panda

J

CC

Panda-Panda

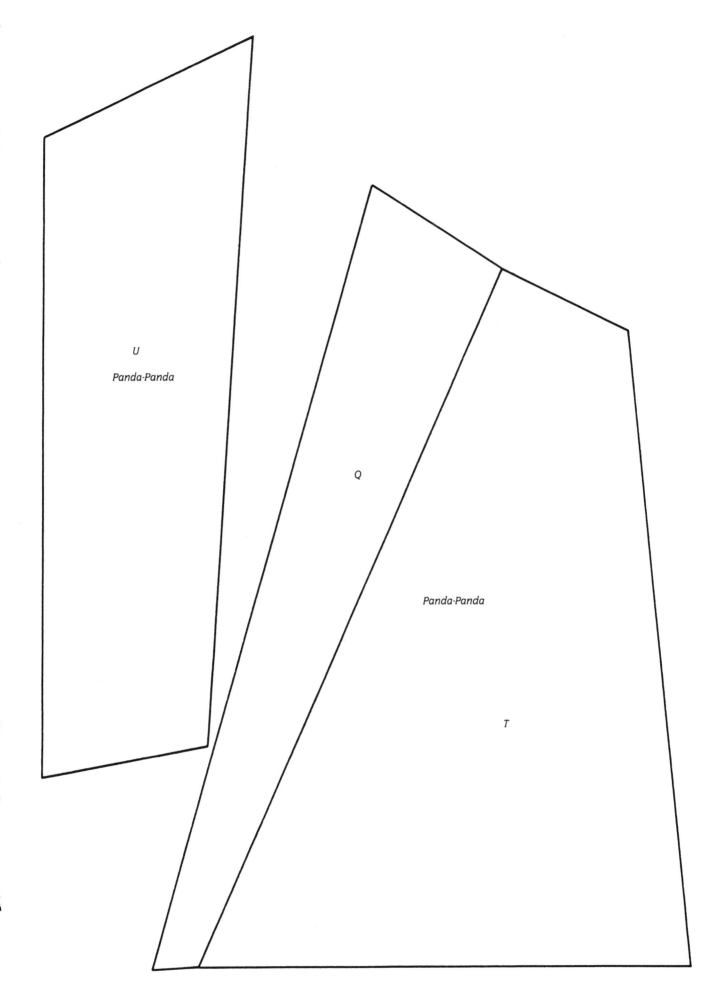

U

Panda-Panda

Q

Panda-Panda

T

113

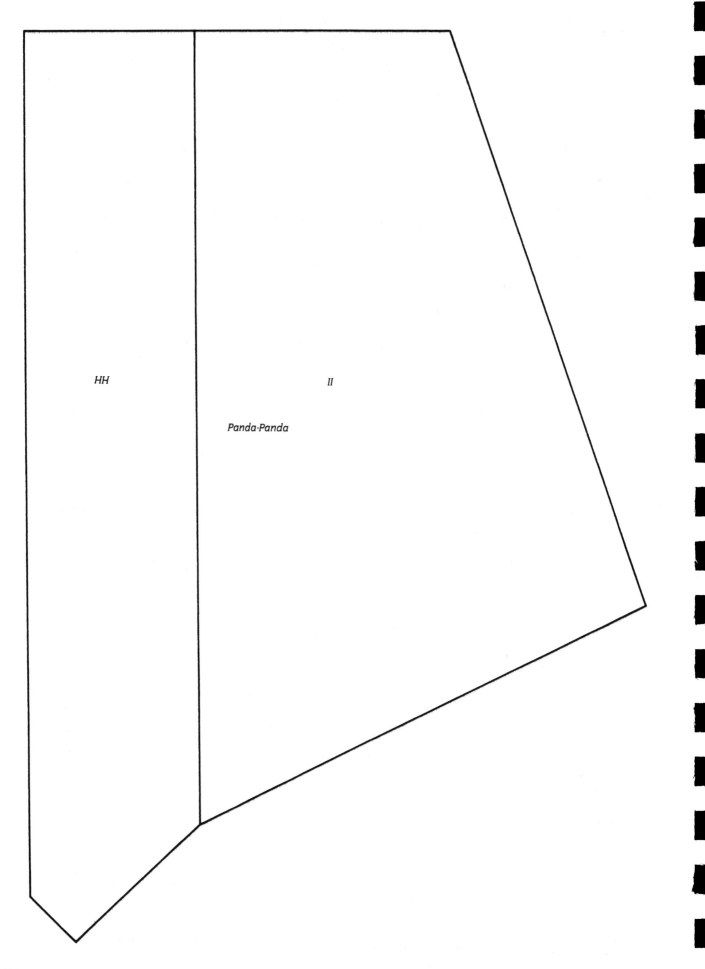

HH

II

Panda·Panda

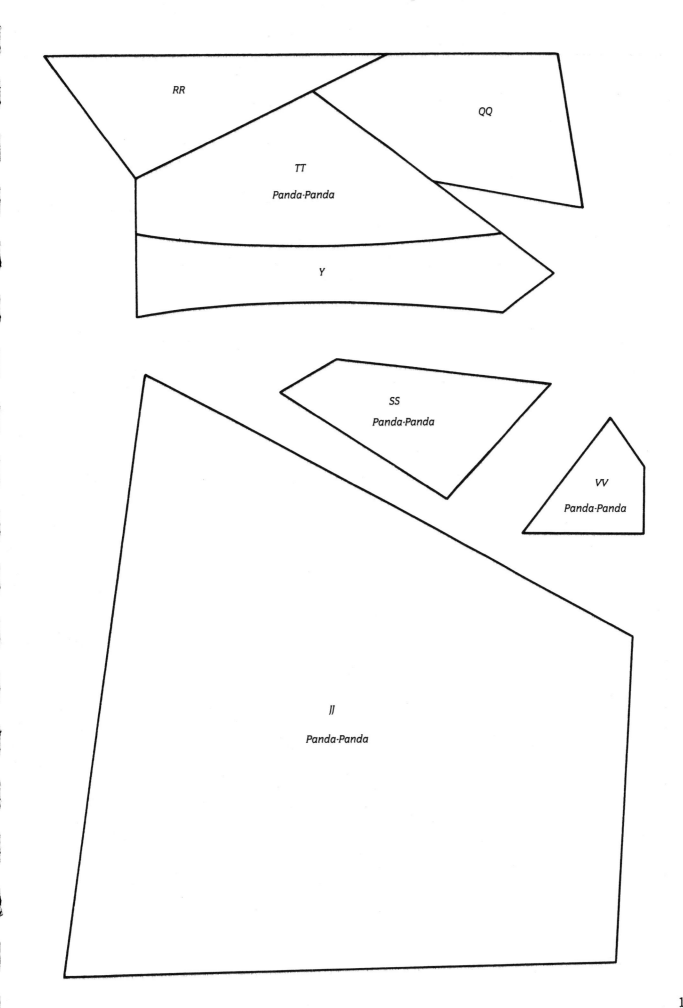

RR

QQ

TT

Panda-Panda

Y

SS
Panda-Panda

VV

Panda-Panda

JJ

Panda-Panda

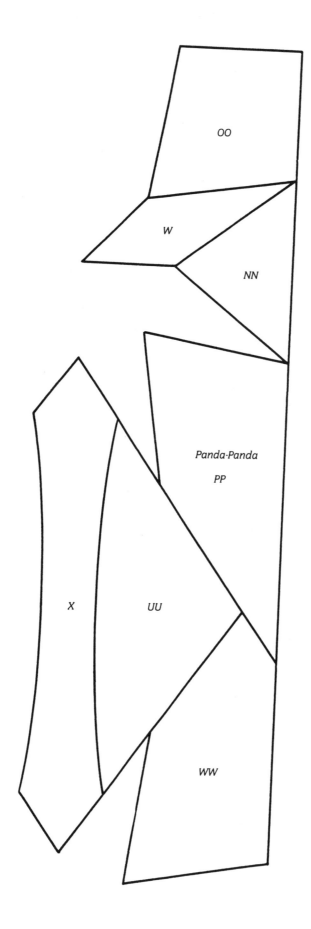

OO

W

NN

Panda-Panda

PP

X

UU

WW

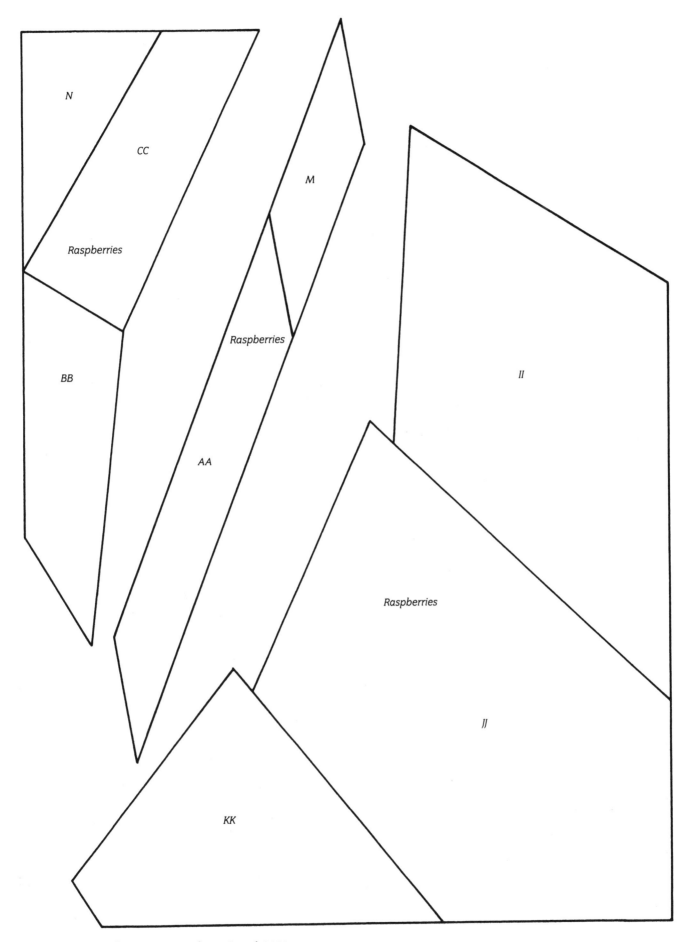

Add ¼" seam allowances to patches A-Q and AA-LL.

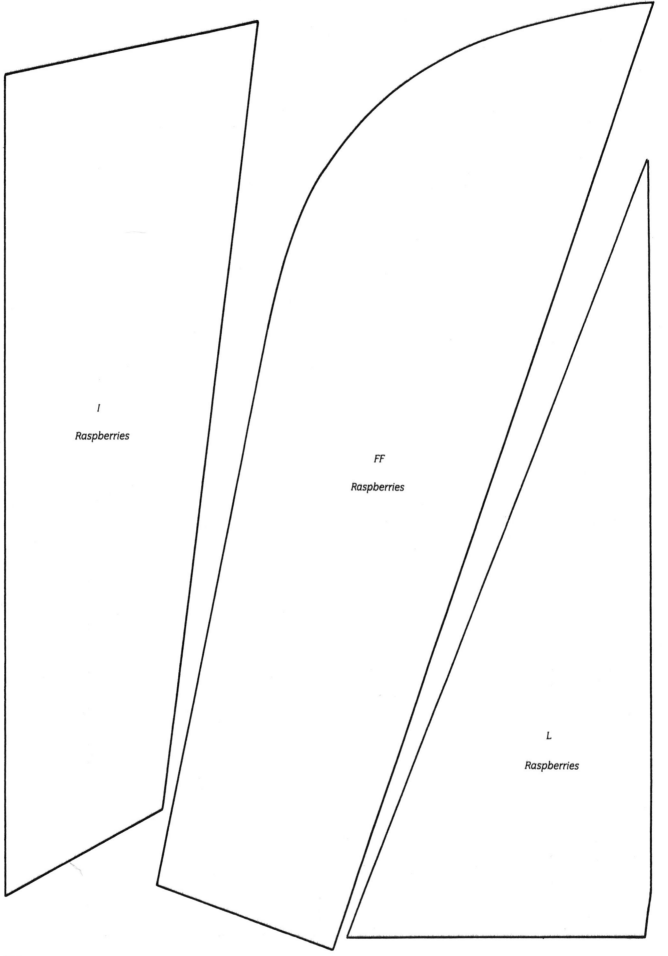

I

Raspberries

FF

Raspberries

L

Raspberries

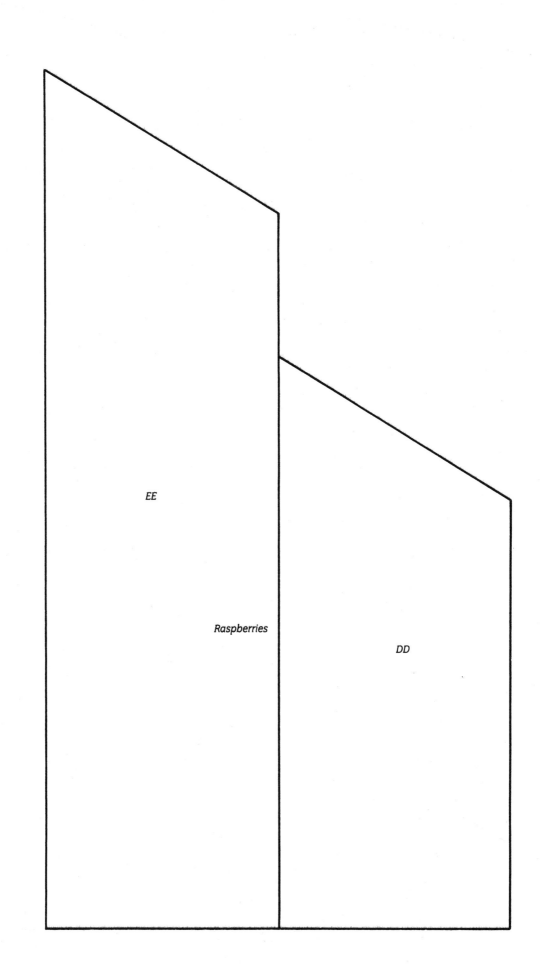

EE

Raspberries

DD

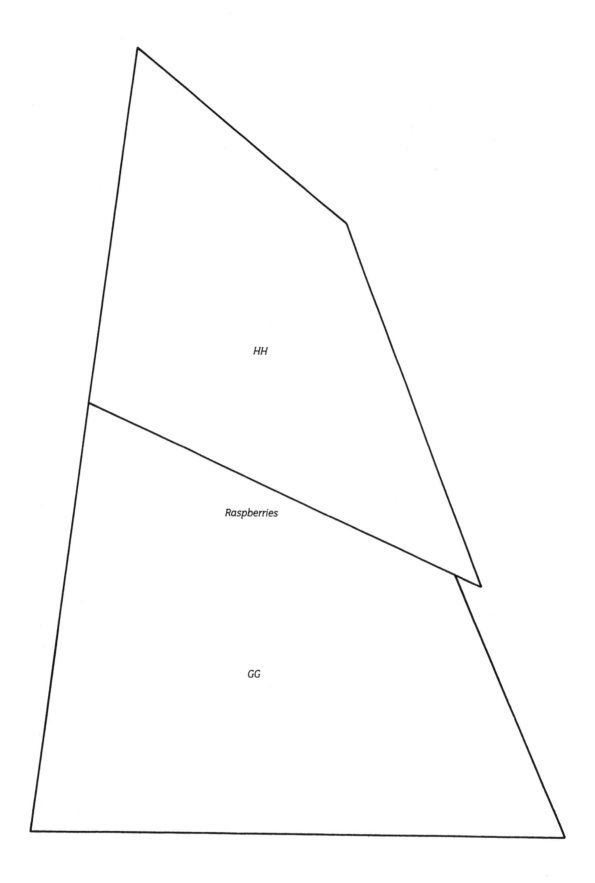

HH

Raspberries

GG

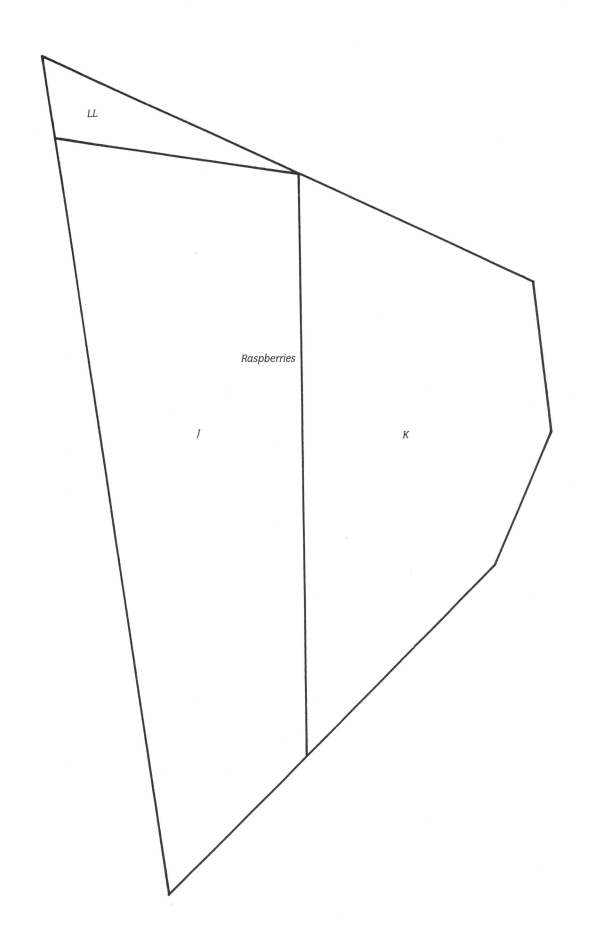

LL

Raspberries

J

K

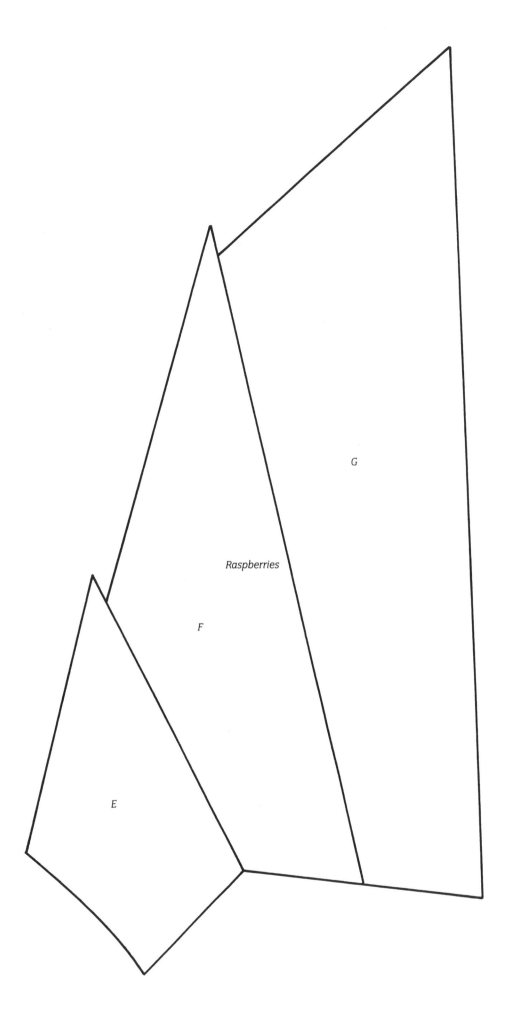

E

F

Raspberries

G

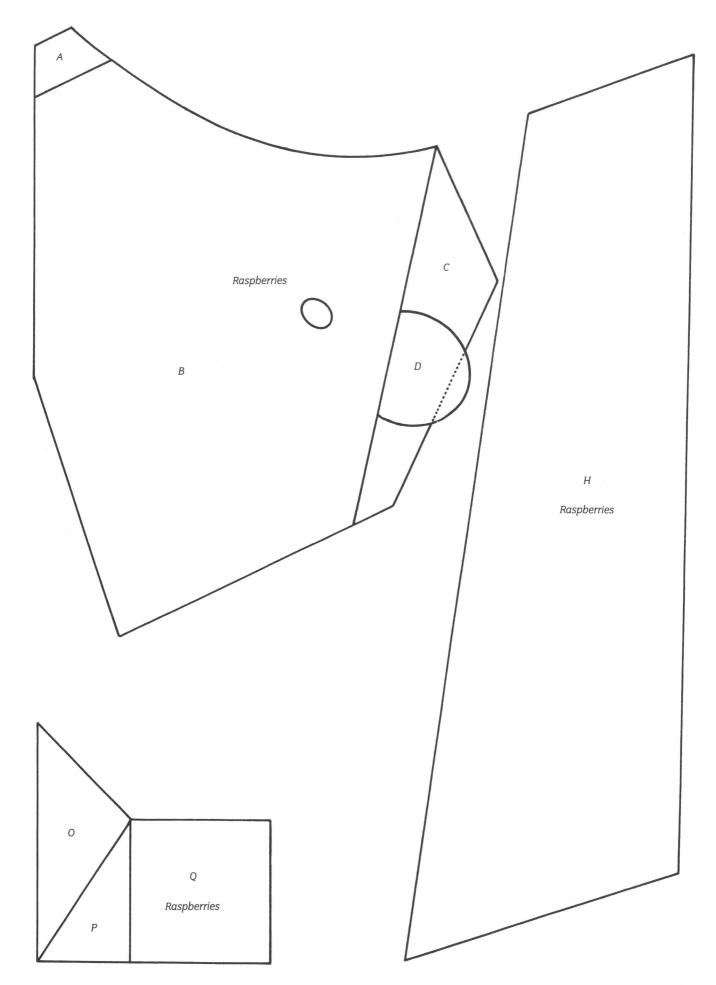

A

Raspberries

B

C

D

H

Raspberries

O

P

Q

Raspberries

123

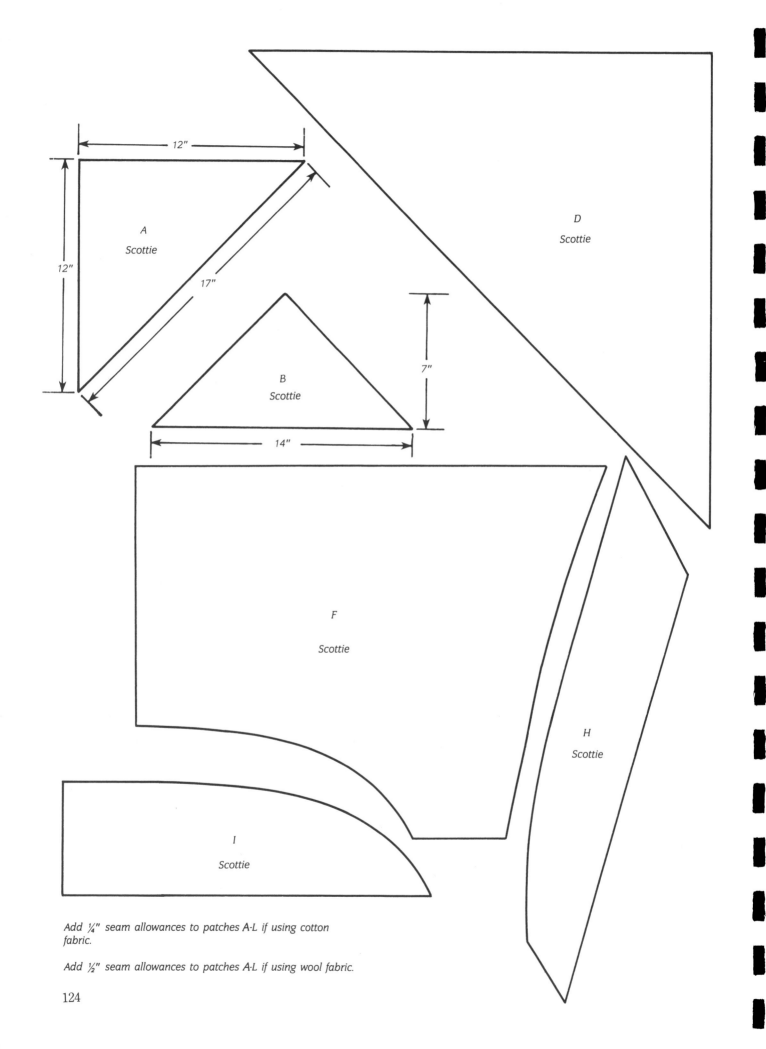

12"

A
Scottie

12"

17"

D
Scottie

B
Scottie

7"

14"

F
Scottie

H
Scottie

I
Scottie

Add ¼" seam allowances to patches A-L if using cotton fabric.

Add ½" seam allowances to patches A-L if using wool fabric.

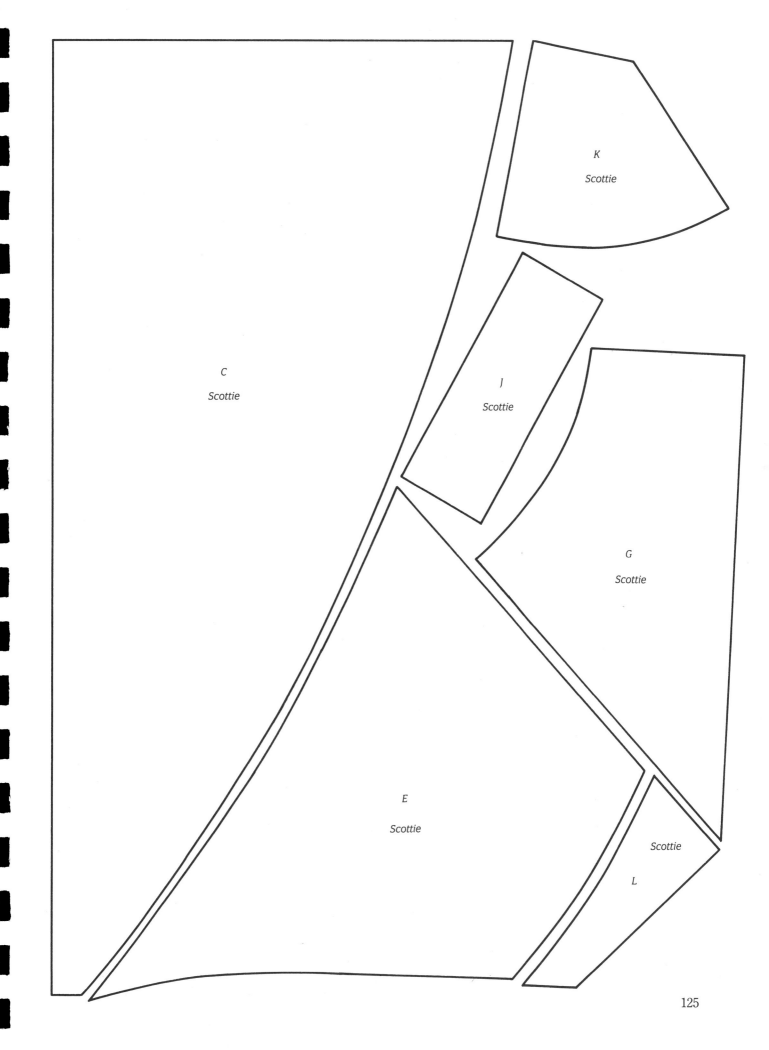

K
Scottie

C
Scottie

J
Scottie

G
Scottie

E
Scottie

Scottie

L

125

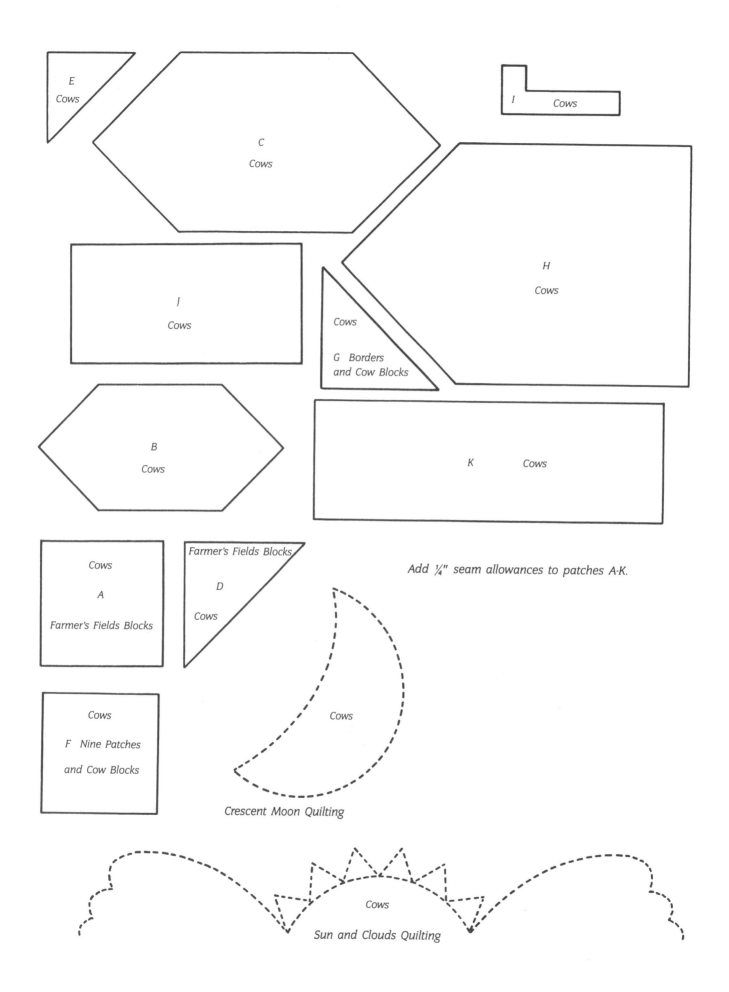

E
Cows

C
Cows

I Cows

J
Cows

H
Cows

Cows

G Borders
and Cow Blocks

B
Cows

K Cows

Cows

A

Farmer's Fields Blocks

Farmer's Fields Blocks

D

Cows

Add ¼" seam allowances to patches A-K.

Cows

F Nine Patches

and Cow Blocks

Cows

Crescent Moon Quilting

Cows

Sun and Clouds Quilting

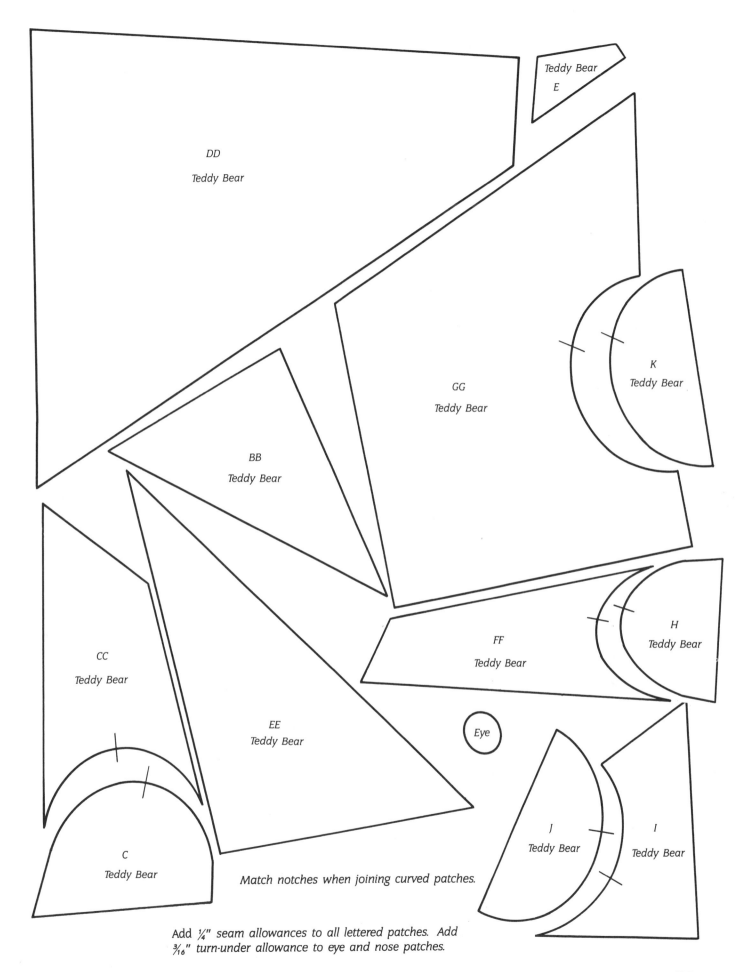

DD
Teddy Bear

Teddy Bear
E

GG
Teddy Bear

BB
Teddy Bear

K
Teddy Bear

CC
Teddy Bear

EE
Teddy Bear

FF
Teddy Bear

H
Teddy Bear

Eye

C
Teddy Bear

J
Teddy Bear

I
Teddy Bear

Match notches when joining curved patches.

Add ¼" seam allowances to all lettered patches. Add
3⁄16" turn-under allowance to eye and nose patches.

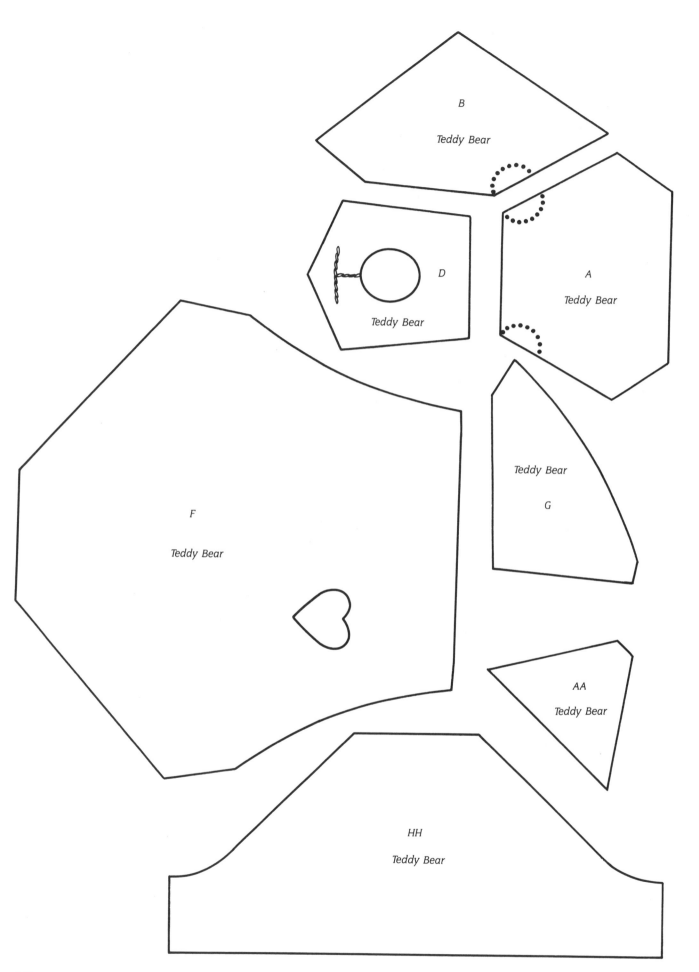

B

Teddy Bear

D

Teddy Bear

A

Teddy Bear

Teddy Bear

G

F

Teddy Bear

AA

Teddy Bear

HH

Teddy Bear

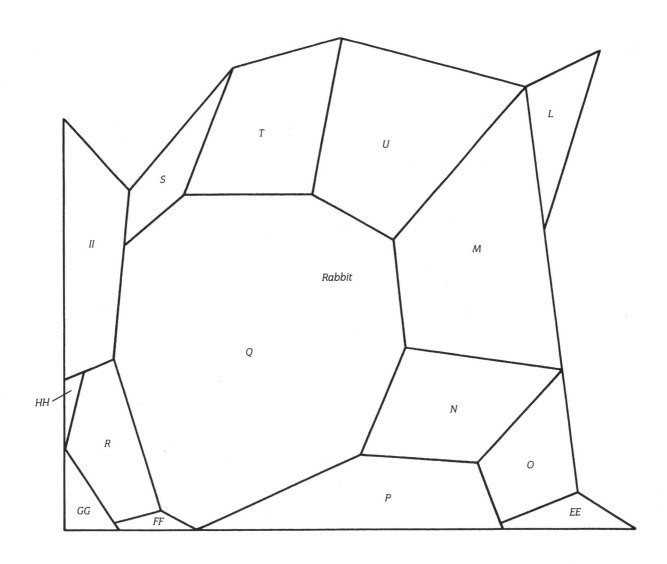

Rabbit

Border square

Add ¼" seam allowances to patches A-Z, a-e, AA-WW, and border square patch. Add ⅛" turn-under allowance to eyes.

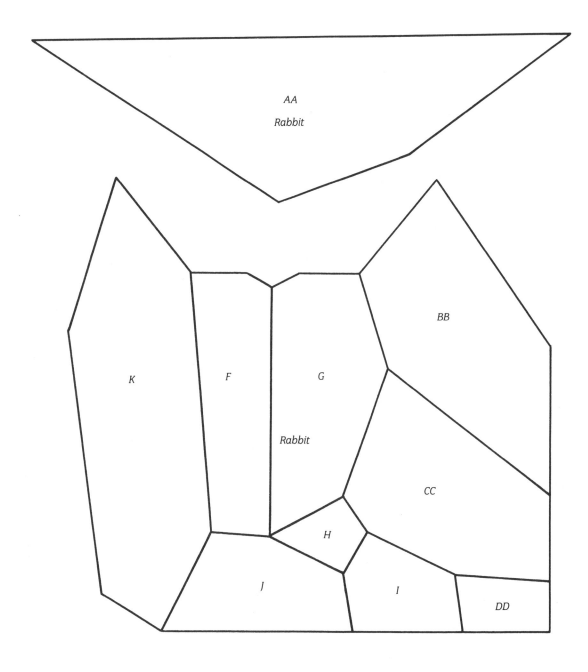

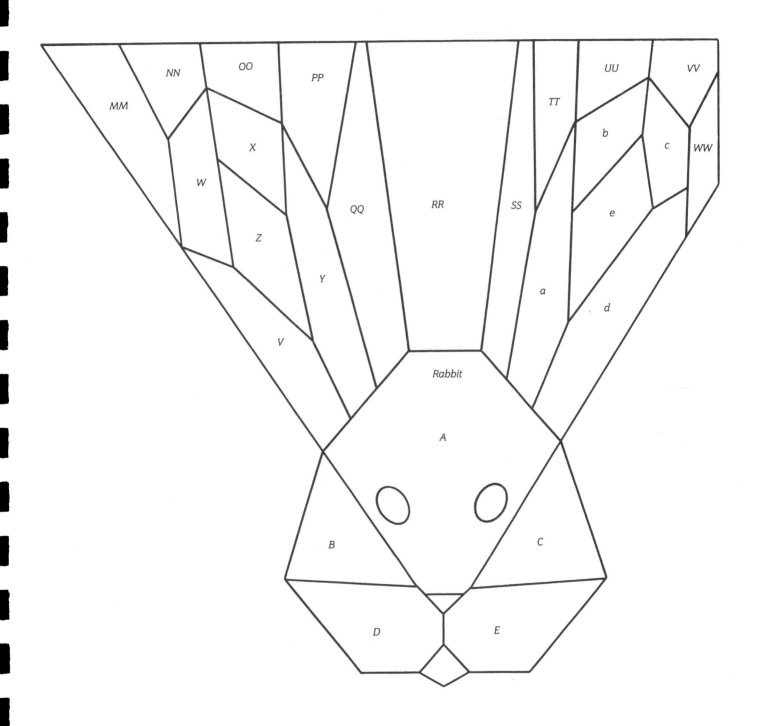

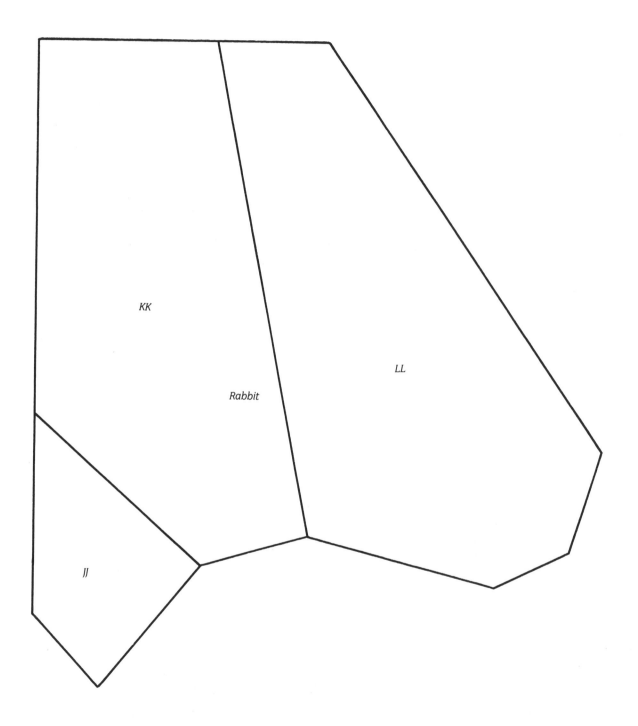

KK

LL

Rabbit

JJ

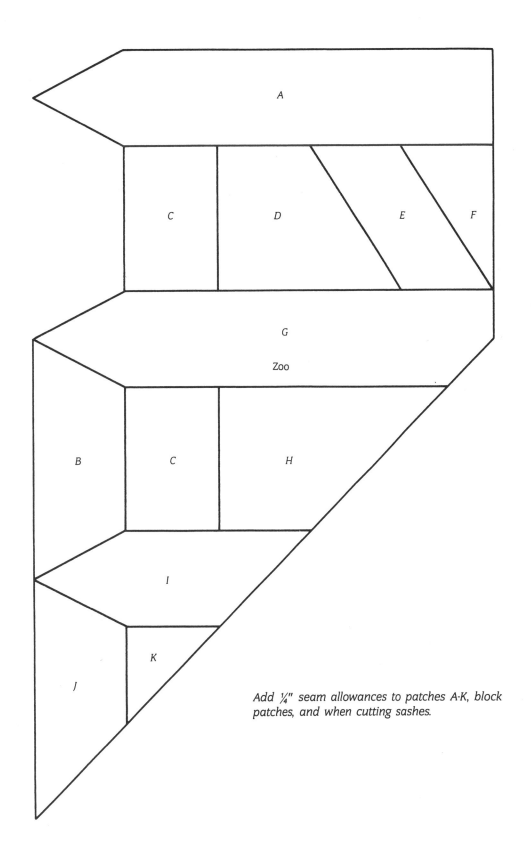

A

C

D

E

F

G

Zoo

B

C

H

I

K

J

Add ¼" seam allowances to patches A-K, block patches, and when cutting sashes.

About the Authors

Marie Shirer and Barbara Brackman first met across the counter of Marie's needlework and quilt shop in Lawrence, Kansas. Barbara sold copies of her *Encyclopedia of Pieced Quilt Patterns* to Marie, who sold fabric and quilting supplies to Barbara. This was the start of a long friendship and many cooperative ventures.

In 1982 Marie moved to Arvada, Colorado, to join the staff of *Quilter's Newsletter Magazine*, where she is Associate Editor. She enjoys living in the foothills of the Rocky Mountains with her Welsh Corgi, Sadie.

Barbara still lives in Lawrence with her English Setter, Spot, and husband James Holmes. She is a free-lance writer and Contributing Editor for *QNM*.